be yourself
improve
yourself

(It's an attitude thing!)

matt booth

Be Yourself; Improve Yourself by Matt Booth

Book Design: Bryce Parks
Cover Design: Andrew Welyczko
Publisher: BHC Publishing
Copy Edited: Peggy Dolson
Project Editor: Suzanne Wright

BHC Publishing, Dubuque, Iowa, U.S.A.
www.bhcpublishing.com

www.beyourselfimproveyourself.com
www.mattbooth.com

First Printing: April 2012

ISBN: 978-098277-72-2-0

This book is dedicated to my beautiful and extremely supportive wife, Joie; our wonderfully entertaining sons, Carter and Graham, who bring us crazy joy every day; and Grandma and Grandpa Kennedy.

Also, to my friend Susan "Deuce" Beecher who continues to inspire me everyday. Miss you.

Table of Contents

Attitude   1

Business 47

Language 77

Personal 107

Introduction

I have a belief. I profoundly believe that I deserve to be happy and successful and that I have the ability to handle anything life throws at me. Furthermore, I profoundly believe that you deserve to be happy and successful and you have the ability to handle anything life throws at you. The million dollar question...do you believe it?

To be happy, you're going to have to be yourself. There is no other way. It is impossible to be happy trying to be someone you're not. Your actions need to originate from who you are rather than from some superficial place. Rediscover your passions and desires. What did you want to be as a kid? Find your uniqueness and use it to serve others and the world will make a place for you. To be successful, you must be in a continued state of self improvement. Make it your mission to be the best you can. You can't help others until you first help yourself. If you're going to lift someone up, you must be on higher ground. If you're not continually improving, you will find it tough to be successful.

By being yourself and improving each day, you will without a doubt have a positive attitude. Just having a positive attitude isn't everything; however, I think it is the start of everything. Being positive ranks highest priority over your skills, talent, experience, education or intelligence. Your attitude is what drives you and determines how high you will rise. Exercise the most important choice given to us as members of the human race and choose to have a positive attitude because it is key to your happiness and success.

This book is designed to be read in short chunks and in no particular order. Feel free to flip around from chapter to chapter. It is full of concise and easy to follow tips to help you be happy and successful. I want you to find one good idea in this book and implement it immediately. So open it up, find one good idea and get started today!

Be Yourself; Improve Yourself

What is leadership? That's a complex question. The best definition of leadership I've found comes from Jim Rohn. He said, "Leadership is the challenge to be something better than average." If you want to be a leader, you must be better than average. There are two rules to be better than average, Be Yourself and Improve Yourself.

Rule number one, Be Yourself. To be better than average, you're going to have to be yourself. There is no other way. It is impossible to be better than mediocre trying to be something you're not. Your actions need to originate from who you are rather than a superficial place. Rediscover your passions and desires. What did you want to be as a kid? Is it even close to what you do for a living? Why not? Find your uniqueness and use it to serve others. Use your gifts to serve others and the world will make a place for you. Be Yourself.

Rule number two, Improve Yourself. To stay above average, you must be in a continued state of self-improvement. Make it your mission to be the best you can. You can't help others until you first help yourself. If you're going to lift someone up, you must be on higher ground. Being better than average is not about ego, it's about helping. If you're not better than average in your personal and professional life, you can't help people. Be a better than average friend, spouse, parent, and business person. Find your uniqueness and constantly improve upon it. Great leaders love what they do and continue learning. Do what you love and Improve Yourself.

To be a leader, you must be better than average. Find your uniqueness, use it to serve others and improve.

e.e. cummings put it like this, "To be nobody but yourself in a world which is doing its best, night and day, to make you everybody else means to fight the hardest battle which any human being can fight; and never stop fighting." To be better than average, Be Yourself; Improve Yourself.

Mattitude Must Dos

As I travel the country and the world doing programs and giving speeches, people always ask me what the most important topics I talk about are. So I've compiled a list of Mattitude "Must Dos".

Be Yourself

Make the commitment to be yourself. Find your uniqueness and use it to serve others. Focus your energy on being yourself and you will be happy. The amazing part is, when you do this, you cannot fail.

Improve Yourself

Improve yourself like your life depends on it, because it does. The cornerstone of success is lifelong self improvement. You are either living or dying a little more each day. If you're improving, you're living.

Check Your Attitude

Your attitude determines your thoughts and your thoughts ultimately determine your destiny. Your success (or lack of) is determined by your attitude.

Smile

Smiling is the ultimate gesture. It's the universal language and almost never misunderstood. A smile, regardless of your age, culture, ethnicity, financial status, faith, or nationality, is understood. Next to breathing, smiling is the most important thing you can do.

Make Eye Contact

Eye contact is the quickest and easiest way to make a connection. Eye contact shows confidence and builds above any other communication tool. Eye contact is unequaled in importance.

Take Risks

Although you're chancing loss, risk is necessary to make progress. A risk must be taken to learn, feel, change, grow, love, and live. You cannot avoid pain and suffering by never taking a risk. If you never risk anything, you'll never accomplish anything.

Actively Listen

Active listening improves mutual understanding. Always remember what Grandma said, "You've got two ears and one mouth. Listen twice as much as you talk."

Be Responsible

We all make mistakes and it's very convenient to deny responsibility. Take responsibility for your actions, learn something, and move on. Don't play the blame game.

Be Clear

Clear communication is vital to success. If you desire to gain people's interest, agreement, and help, be as clear as possible. A confused mind always says no.

Believe Body Language

Body Language is the unspoken communication that occurs in every encounter. Over 1/2 of your total message is communicated through body language. Be very aware of body language; your own and of others.

Use Your Internal GPS

Your "gut feeling" helps guide your decisions and actions. Your body gives you a tremendous amount of useful, intuitive information. That "gut feeling" or "hunch" is one of the most valuable and under used skills in the human tool box.

80/20 Rule

In 1906, Italian economist Vilfredo Pareto created a mathematical formula to describe the unequal distribution of wealth in his country, observing that 20% of the people owned 80% of the wealth. The 80/20 Rule suggests that 20% of the causes account for 80% of the results. In sales, for example — 20% of the salespeople sell 80% of the product. In a service club — 20% of the people do 80% of the work. By the office water cooler — 20% of the people do 80% of the complaining. The 80/20 Rule works and has been applied to almost everything around. Almost everything, except people's attitudes, that's where I come in.

The 80/20 Rule applied to attitudes says — 20% of the people are responsible for 80% of the positive attitudes. I'll say that 20% of people have a positive attitude 80% of the time or more. Eighty percent of people are only positive 20% of the time. That means that only 2 out of 10 people are mostly positive (80% or more). The other 8 are less positive, totaling only 20% of the time.

Let's test the 80/20 Rule as it applies to attitudes. I want you to write down the names of the 5 people with which you spend the most time. Go ahead, jot down their names. There is even a place to write them in the book. You can't use pets either; they are not people. After you have those 5 people, assign a percentage to each person's attitude.

Name _____ _____%

Name _____ _____%

Name _____ _____%

Name _____ _____%

Name _____ _____%

Are they mostly positive or mostly negative? Mostly Positive = 80% or higher. Mostly Negative = 20% or less.

Do you spend the majority of your time with people who are mostly positive or mostly negative? Do their attitudes influence you? I'll bet there is 1 person on your list that is mostly positive and the other 4 are mostly negative. Isn't that the 80/20 Rule? Look around and see for yourself if the 80/20 Rule applies to attitudes.

I believe attitude is a choice! I also believe you deserve to be happy and successful. If you are mostly positive, you are already happy and successful. Congratulations! If you are mostly negative, you have the ability to change that. Attitude is a choice. Can you imagine what your life would look like if you went from being mostly negative to mostly positive? The 80/20 Rule should serve as a daily reminder to you that your attitude is your choice.

Attitude Is Everything

You've heard the old saying that attitude is everything. Have you ever wondered why is attitude everything? The answer, your attitude determines your thoughts and your thoughts determine who you are. Understanding that you have the power to choose your attitude is essential. Your attitude influences what you think about events today and is the foundation that builds the events you will experience tomorrow. Attitude is everything!

You must be aware of your attitude and manage it at all times. Your attitude can combat anger, frustration, and disappointment. Your attitude determines your self-image. Attitude is a critical factor in your success in life. Your attitude can determine your level of success more than the skills and training you have received. Your attitude determines your thinking; and you have the power to choose your attitude. By choosing your attitude, you can choose to be happy right now doing whatever it is that you are doing. Attitude is everything!

Your mind is like your computer. It doesn't judge what you input; it simply accepts it as reality. Your attitude determines how you react to that input. The good news about that is you choose your attitude! That choice determines your perception (understanding). Your perception becomes reality and ultimately determines how you see the world around you (happy or sad, positive or negative). It is imperative to understand that you choose your attitude. Attitude is everything!

By your attitude, you decide to be yourself and improve yourself. By your attitude, you decide to take action or not take action. By your attitude, you decide to try or give up. By your own attitude you and you alone actually decide whether to succeed or fail. Your future depends upon your attitude. It is not what happens to you that determines your future; it is your attitude toward what happens. Your attitude determines thoughts, and your thoughts determine who you are. Attitude is everything!

Can-Do Attitude

A can-do attitude sets the achievers apart from the dreamers. If you have a can-do attitude, you believe that by setting your mind to something, it is possible to achieve. Someone with a can-do attitude focuses on what can be done rather than what can't be done. A can-doer is willing to do whatever it takes to cross the finish line. Understand that your attitude makes the difference and you'll discover that nearly anything is possible.

Having a can-do attitude is the difference between success and failure. It plays a part in every phase of your life and is particularly important when you face a difficult or seemingly hopeless situation. There are many ways to look at a situation. Can-doers look for what they can do; others look for what can't be done. One of the worst human habits is a tendency to concentrate on what can't be done rather than what can. In life, as in sports, there is a huge difference in focusing on "not losing" instead of focusing on "winning." By spending time and energy on what can't be done, you erode your confidence and chip away at your abilities. Look beyond the "can't" of a situation and find the "can."

Can-doers initiate action and are willing to put forth the effort and pay the price of success. When others are overwhelmed and feel helpless, can-doers continue pressing forward. Achievement comes to many people not because they are exceptional, but because they have a can-do attitude. A can-do attitude tremendously strengthens skills, talent, experience, education, and intelligence. You can't do anything to change the fact that problems exist. You can however, overcome those problems and reach your goals with a can-do attitude. A can-do attitude also sets the achievers apart from the mere dreamers. A can-do attitude doesn't guarantee success, but it gives you a fighting chance.

Cover Your Bowl

Have you ever felt like someone is peeing in your bowl of Cheerios? Is someone with a bad attitude bringing you down? Do you know someone who needs an attitude adjustment? It's easy to see the difference between a negative and positive attitude in someone else. Before letting people ruin your day, cover your bowl.

Your attitude is the benchmark of success (or lack of it). A positive attitude will make a profound difference. It is that important. Checking your attitude (CYA) should not be a one-time event taking place on the 1st of January each year. You should CYA at least as often as you brush your teeth. You probably brush your teeth when you get up in the morning and when you go to bed. By checking your attitude often, you can recognize warning signs of negativity, blame, and pessimism and replace them by being positive, responsible, and optimistic. You wouldn't think of only brushing your teeth once a year. Heck, you probably wouldn't think of leaving the house without brushing your teeth. You shouldn't leave the house without checking your attitude.

Checking your attitude is hard work. It's much easier to be negative than it is to be positive. Just look at the people around you for proof. To CYA, you have to be brutally honest with yourself and take full responsibility.

You must fight, kick, claw, and do whatever is necessary to check your attitude. You are the only one who can change your attitude. Be accountable for who you are and how you behave. The attitude you hold aligns with the role you play in life. If you don't like the role you are playing, check your attitude.

Regardless of your IQ or number of degrees, much of your success (or lack of) is determined by your attitude. Education is worthwhile; a good attitude is priceless. There is really very little difference between people, but that little difference makes a big difference. The little difference is attitude. The big difference is whether it is negative or positive. Life is better when you have a good attitude. If you check your attitude as often as you brush your teeth, you won't have to worry about covering your @*#%!. The most successful people in the world are human beings just like you who check their attitudes and brush their teeth. If they can do it, you can too. Check Your Attitude.

Get Off the Fence Day

I know there are compelling reasons for riding the fence. Which reasons are you using today? Are you overwhelmed, powerless or tired? Did you run out of time? Maybe you're waiting for someone to help you down off of the fence? Whatever the reason, you're still on the fence about something. Today is Get Off the Fence Day because success comes to you when you decide to do just that, get off the fence.

You know when you're "fence riding." It happens all of the time. It can be small decisions like chicken or beef, Budweiser or Guinness, country or hip hop. Maybe it's a big decision like quitting your job, filing for divorce, or changing hairstylist. (Have you ever tried to break up with a hairstylist?) Choosing to do nothing (riding the fence) is just about the worst decision you can make. Decide what you are going to do and do it. Right or wrong, you'll be further ahead by getting off of the fence.

It's not always easy to make a decision, and no matter what you choose, you may wonder if you did the right thing. Anytime you make a decision, you run the risk of making a mistake. Who cares if you screw-up? It is part of the process.

Use this quick process to make a decision:

1. Understand — interpret the situation to the best of your ability

2. Decide — make a decision

3. Take Action — follow through with your decision

4. Pay Attention — learn from each decision

Fence riding is exhausting and unproductive. It's momentum breaking, demoralizing, and impedes progress. Understand the situation, make a decision, take action, and learn from your mistakes. There is no better time than today to Get Off the Fence! Success comes to you when you do just that.

How to Change Your Attitude

It is your attitude, not your aptitude, which is the key to your success. Unfortunately, no one is born with a positive attitude. It is a skill that is learned over time that becomes a way of life. Sure, everyone has bad moments and that is why it is vital to CYA (Check Your Attitude) daily. Your attitude is the very soul of who you are. No matter what you've been through, no matter how many times you've stumbled, you choose your attitude. Here are some techniques that will help you choose a positive attitude and refuse to be affected by negativity.

Be Yourself

To make having a positive attitude a way of life, you first must be yourself. If you are always trying to be someone else, you're not very good at it and it gets very tiring. To have a positive attitude, be yourself.

Improve Yourself

Read books, articles, magazines that help you understand and adopt the attitude you desire. Watch films or listen to music or CDs that inspire you and encourage you.

Choice

Recognize your choices. Regardless of what has happened to you in the past or what will happen to you in the future, you choose your attitude.

Thoughts

Change your thoughts and you change your attitude. Use positive thoughts to create a new perspective for yourself. Just by changing your thoughts, you can change your attitude and thereby change your behavior.

Words

Listen to yourself. Are your words positive or negative? As goofy as it may sound, try starting each day with positive and upbeat words. Your words become actions.

People

Find some role models and imitate them. After you do that, be a role model for someone else. Avoid negative people as much as possible. They suck the life out of you.

Goals

If someone else is rowing your boat, it goes where they want it to. Start rowing your own boat. If you don't have your own goals, you'll spend your entire life helping others accomplish theirs.

Change

Embrace change. Do things differently and you start thinking differently. Change your actions and your environment. Make your environment reflect the attitude you desire.

Body Language

Picture the body language of a person with a positive attitude. They exude optimism. What does your body language exude?

Solutions

Focus on solutions — not on problems. If you focus on solutions, you cannot wallow in problems, complaining, blaming, or moaning.

Be Assertive

If you don't like what someone else is doing or saying, tell them. Assert your feelings and beliefs instead of becoming angry, combative, or passive.

It Is What It Is

Figure out which problems you can solve (I need to lose 10 pounds) and which problems are beyond your control (the price of gas). Work on accepting the things you can't change. Learn to say "It is what it is."

If I Learn Just One Thing

Have you ever gone to a class or training program and thought to yourself, "learn just one thing?" If I learn just one thing — all of the time, effort, and investment would be worth it. Learning just one thing isn't difficult. There is no shortage of good ideas. And yes, just one thing is all it takes. Learning just one thing and using it can change your life.

Learning does not stop when you leave the classroom. It is a continual investment in your future. The practice of learning is what makes you human and life worthwhile. Make it your mission to learn. In fact, successful people became successful by consistently learning and applying just one thing at a time. It gives you perspective, helps you adapt, keeps you edgy, helps you grow, deepens your character, makes you rich, and gives you confidence.

Good ideas are everywhere, look around. There is no shortage of good ideas. Search out opportunities to learn. You can learn from another person, a book, a class, a seminar or training. Go idea hunting everyday. If you stay alert, you can learn anywhere from anyone.

Remember, self-improvement does not stop when you leave the classroom. Imagine what you can do by learning and applying just one thing each day? It moves you forward. When you learn, you get better. When you get better, the people around you get better. Continual improvement gives you the edge. It's the learning of new skills, new concepts, and new experiences that can change your life. Learn just one thing!

Inside the Box

Were you told to "think outside of the box" today? People use this catchphrase to encourage others to look at a challenge from a new perspective. It often comes from someone in charge who feels the current solutions or ideas are just not good enough. The cliché loosely means "think creatively." "Think outside of the box" has become the least creative way to tell someone to be more creative.

The phrase "think outside of the box" first began at the Disney organization in the 1950's. Thinking outside of the box represented Walt Disney's vision. After Walt's death in 1966, everyone would ask, "What would Walt do (WWWD)?" The leaders would then explain that Walt's thought process was "thinking outside of the box," referring to his: thinking creatively, not accepting the status quo, openness to new ideas, and willingness to explore.

Today, the phrase has become as common as Mickey Mouse. Every day is filled with this cliché. It rolls off of the tongues of leaders, bosses, and politicians. I've heard it in church and in advertisements, "Think outside of the bun." I have a friend that tells everyone that he wants to be cremated when he dies because he has spent his whole life thinking outside of the box, and he sure doesn't want to be buried in one.

When someone tells you to think outside of the box, they are trying to get you to think creatively and pushing you to do more for the company, team, organization, and/or yourself, right?

It is one of the most overused phrases. Does it really enhance creativity? When I hear someone say we must "think outside the box," I want to ask them to think of a more creative way to tell me to think creatively. It is almost to the point where just saying "think outside the box," actually closes the box.

"Think outside of the box" has lost its zing! It is the least creative way to tell someone to be more creative. If Walt Disney were still alive, I bet he would ban his employees from saying "think outside the box." He would have thought of 48 other ways to say be more creative by now. If everyone is thinking outside the box, maybe the best way to think creatively is to "think inside the box?"

Letter to My Godson

Heroism is the quality of using strength to overcome obstacles toward a noble goal. It's often associated with the feats of heroes like Superman or Wonder Woman. These heroes go on great, dangerous adventures to right wrongs and make the world a better place. Any noble accomplishment in life will be full of danger, risk, and uncertainty. Heroes don't always stop bad criminals or save the world from destruction, but they do overcome danger, risk, and uncertainty. This list will help you live in heroic fashion.

Be Yourself. Every person has unique talents and the ability to develop them. Unfortunately, many people never discover, or fail to develop, their talents. You should work harder on developing yourself than you do on anything else. Identify your uniqueness, use it to serve others and the world will make a place for you.

Improve Yourself. Be in a continual state of self-improvement. Make it your mission to be the best you can. Improve yourself like your life depends on it — because it does. Self improvement allows you to be a better friend, spouse, parent, and businessperson.

Choose Your Attitude. Understanding that you have the power to choose your attitude is essential. Your attitude determines your thoughts and what you think about today is the foundation that builds the events you will experience tomorrow. Attitude is the critical factor in your success. Your attitude will determine your level of success in developing new skills.

Listen and Learn. Always be ready to find wisdom in what other people say, and try very hard to absorb it. Almost everyone you meet will have some interesting know-how or expertise. Go through life attempting to learn those unique qualities in the people you meet. Assume that the average person you meet has much to teach you, and be ready to drink it in.

Expect Good Things. The world is full of strange and wonderful people. You'll find most think they are well-meaning and good. There is good and bad in most people, but if you treat everyone as if he's a good person; you'll tend to bring out the good. Conversely, if you treat people like they're bad, not only will they clash with you, but you will also help them to become bad. People have a tendency to become exactly what you expect of them.

Take Action. There are three types of people in this world: those who make things happen, those who watch things happen, and those who say "what just happened? Take action to make things happen.

Your journey will be full of danger, risk, and uncertainty. You may very well end up fighting for freedom and righting wrongs. Perhaps you will help others achieve greatness by being a wonderful person and loyal friend. In the end, if you approach life in a heroic fashion, you will be successful.

Manage Your Attitude

You might not realize this, but you are responsible for managing your attitude. It is critical to success. If you don't manage your attitude, who will? Manage your attitude just like you manage your career, your money, your house, and your family. It is of utmost importance. Life is better when you manage your attitude.

Have you ever heard the statement, "That person needs an attitude adjustment"? It seems easy to recognize someone else's bad attitude — and not so easy to recognize your own. Ask a few good friends or family members, "On a scale of one to 10, how is my attitude most days?" Their answers will help you determine your attitude. Their answers may also surprise you. Your attitude is vital to people around you and crucial in your self-improvement and personal advancement. If you're not managing your attitude, you're leaving it to chance. Your attitude is way too important to leave to chance.

Regardless of the number of college credits or degrees you have, your success is determined by your attitude. Your attitude is a learned skill that can be managed by understanding where it comes from and taking control of where it is going. To manage your attitude, you must first be aware and then take responsibility for it. After that, you'll need the willingness to change it.

Your attitude is a huge part of your life. It can determine what you can do and where you go. Learning how to manage your attitude is an important step toward taking control of your life. The same way you manage other aspects of your life, you must start managing your attitude. Life is better when you can manage your attitude. Move from mediocre to magnificent by managing your attitude.

Near-Life Experience

Life isn't too short, it's just that most people wait too long to begin.

You've heard about people who have survived near-death experiences and the incredible impact it can have. A near-death experience can change values, beliefs, and attitudes. Don't wander through life almost living and don't wait for a near-death experience to really begin living. Start making your life really count now.

You are stuck in a near-life experience when you feel that real life will happen next month or next year. There are thousands of reasons people use that prevent them from really living — fear of the unknown, family responsibilities, economic uncertainty, poor self-confidence, and on and on. You're having a near life experience if — you're just working to retire, if you've always wanted to coach little league but haven't, if you're making a bunch of money and are not happy. You need to check your attitude and really start living.

Just recently, I've been close to a near-death experience and a near-life experience. The long-term results of both these experiences are undetermined. A close friend was in a terrible car accident. Hopefully, she's going to be just fine and will use this near-death experience to really start living. I also had a person in a seminar that was stuck in a near-life experience. Here is what he had to say after my seminar, "Starting Friday after your session, I decided that I will have control over my attitude, and it has already shown positive results. My two small children recognize how 'happy daddy is' and my wife has appreciated my better mood and willingness to do more around the house. I know it is only Monday, but things are better for me and I know it has to do with my attitude."

These two experiences have made an impact on my life. We shouldn't wait for a near-death experience like a car accident to assess our values, beliefs, and attitudes. We must begin living the life we want to now, because it doesn't automatically get easier or better next month or next year. Don't succumb to one of the thousands of reasons to be stuck in a near-life experience. We must use them as a wake-up call to begin living now.

On a Tenant's Wall

The end of the year always signals a time of reflection and a time to start thinking about New Year's resolutions. What will be on your mind for the upcoming year? It is not only important to write down your thoughts and ideas; you must also constant remind yourself of them. Carry them in your wallet, post them in the bathroom, or next to your bed like this list I found on a tenant's bedroom wall.

1. My future is bright.
2. Retrain my brain to focus on the positive, not the negative.
3. I am strong and can handle whatever life throws my way.
4. Everything happens when it's meant to happen.
5. I choose to love and appreciate myself.
6. I am grateful for the good in life.
7. I can make healthy choices.
8. Happiness lies before me.
9. I forgive my flaws and celebrate my strengths.

If you do not have your plans in writing, then they are just dreams that might come true. Dreams are great until they get crowded out by everything else in your head and in your life. Putting your plans in writing and hanging them next to your bed can make all the difference in the world.

Respond or React

"To respond is positive, to react is negative."

Zig Ziglar

No matter who you are, the never-ending chorus of bad news is enough to test your Positive Mental Attitude (PMA). People everywhere are reacting to low consumer confidence, high unemployment, layoffs and slumping markets. Most recent reactions show people gyrating out of control. Especially in difficult times, it must be understood that a positive attitude is essential. How can you remain positive when everywhere you look there's bad news? Stop reacting and start responding to the environment around you.

Reacting is often an unconscious reflex to a situation or event. It can be a knee-jerk to external stimulus (not to be confused with a stimulus package). The doctor hits your knee with a rubber hammer and your leg jerks. A person reacts when they feel like they have no control over a situation. By reacting, you let events or other people dictate your life. Today's environment is loaded with reports that seem beyond control. Reacting rather than responding to these events only causes more damage.

A response is a thoughtful action to a situation or event. You take in the situation, consider the options, and make a decision that is most sensible. Think of EMTs or Firefighters — they respond, assess the situation, and then take action. When you thoughtfully respond to events, rather than with knee-jerk reactions, you maintain control.

We have experienced circumstances that we would rather not have experienced. Look back at hard times you've made it through — whether it was a failed business venture, failed relationship, or being fired from a job — those hard times helped you discover something more within yourself to create the change you needed. Hard times bring out the best in many people. There will be new ideas, inventions, and businesses started by people who discover more within. Will you respond and be part of the solution or react and hope for the best? It is easy to be positive in good times, but to ingrain a positive attitude into your character, you must practice it in bad times as well. This is a temporary crisis. You can continue reacting or respond and use it as the catalyst that transforms you into a new, more resilient and secure being.

Risk

Risk is simply defined as "exposing oneself to the chance of loss." The amount of risk is considered proportional to the potential loss. The harsher the loss is, the greater the amount of perceived risk. Although you're chancing loss, risk is necessary to make progress. A risk must be taken to learn, feel, change, grow, love, and live. You cannot avoid pain and suffering by never taking a risk. If you never risk anything, you'll never do anything or have anything.

Risk taking happens when you participate in any activity with an uncertain outcome. It is risky to ask someone on a date, invest in the stock market, gamble, volunteer, accept a challenging project, or talk to a friend about a sensitive issue. Each example has an uncertain outcome and a certain level of risk.

Your body recognizes risk and reacts accordingly. Your heart beats wildly, your breathing gets faster, and your blood pressure increases, you will get cotton mouth, your knees will shake uncontrollably, and your stomach feels like you've just eaten at a super greasy diner — depending on the level of risk. Welcome to the discomfort zone! The perception of risk triggers changes in your body that are experienced as pleasant or unpleasant. Whether it is pleasant or unpleasant depends on your tolerance for risk. That is why some people avoid risk and others seek it out.

You were born a risk taker. As a child, you risked your whole world attempting to take your very first steps. You didn't know or care about the consequences. Attempting to walk was necessary to make progress. Falling was the "exposing oneself to the chance of loss" for getting on your feet and moving. You don't remember, but you fell many times before you ever walked. Falling was the price you paid to make progress.

To move forward, you must get used to the fact that you're going to fall — probably quite often. Taking risks may never be comfortable, but it is the price you must pay. Make the decision right now to take more risks. Decide this very moment there will be no more crawling around. You will fall many times, but don't worry, what's significant is that you've taken a risk. Even when you fall, you usually fall forward, and falling forward is progress.

Speaking It Into Existence

There is an old theory that goes, "How You Speak Becomes Your Reality." Are you living this theory right now? Listen to the content of what you say. Do the words you speak match the life you live? There is a very close relationship between the words you speak and the life you live. How you speak becomes your reality.

I know a guy, for example, that hates Mondays. He thinks Mondays "stink." Thinking it isn't enough, he has to tell the whole world how bad Mondays "stink." Nothing ever goes right for him on Mondays, and he wishes they didn't even exist. Week in and week out his Mondays are horrendous. Conversely, the same guy loves Fridays. It is his favorite day of the week and he tells everyone. Is there that big of a difference between Monday and Friday or is he speaking it into existence?

I'll bet your Mondays and your Fridays reflect exactly what you say about them. The world listens and people listen to what you say. If you tell people over and over that Mondays stink, you are simply planting the "Mondays stink" seed. Choose your words carefully. How you speak becomes your reality.

If the content of your words stink, chances are your life stinks. If the content of your words are bright, there is a good chance that your life is bright. Recognize the relationship between the words you speak and the life you live. If you want to change your life, you'll have to make a conscious effort to change how you speak. Try screaming at the top of your lungs how much you love Mondays and see if you can speak that into existence.

The Choice Is Yours

Although most people would have never guessed, for some time, I was in a rut. I was always stuck on the edge of really living. The great things in life were just waiting around the corner. Real life was always about to begin. Regrettably, there were always obstacles in my way, unfinished business and challenges to get through first. I'd catch myself thinking life will be better next month or next year. If I could only get in better shape, finish my degree, get a different job and make more money. Then look out world. I finally figured out that those obstacles and challenges in my life were my life. This easy but not simple change in thinking makes all the difference. You can't just sit around waiting for life to begin. If you want things to change for you, you must change. The choice is yours.

Every time I talk about choice, I'm reminiscent of the movie *Braveheart*. It's the story of William Wallace in his valiant struggle to free Scotland from the oppressive King Edward I of England. It's a story filled with treachery, injustice, betrayal, and courage. At the pinnacle of the movie, Braveheart gives us insight about choice. The Princess of Wales was pleading for his life and begging Wallace to swear allegiance to the King, thereby avoiding a slow and very painful death. She says to Wallace, "If you do not swear allegiance to the King, you will surely die." To which Braveheart responds, "Every man dies, not every man really lives." Everyone dies, but not everyone really lives. The choice is yours.

No matter where you are in life, there will always be someone who is more successful than you and has chosen to be miserable. You will also always be able to find someone who has less than you but has chosen to enjoy life. Real life doesn't begin next month, next year, or when you get your act together. It begins when you decide. Every morning, when you wake up, you have choices; you can choose to be in a good mood, or you can choose to be in a bad mood. Each time something bad happens, you can choose to be a victim, or you can choose to learn from it. Every time someone complains, you can choose to accept their complaining, or you can find the positive. The choice is yours.

Those obstacles and challenges in your life are your life. If you want things to change for you, *you* must change. If you don't make a choice, someone will make it for you. Think the thoughts, have the emotions, and feel the feelings you deserve now. Life is not too short, it's just that most of us wait too long to start living. There is no better time to start living than now. There is only one guarantee. We will all die — but will you really live?

The choice is yours.

The Frog and the Scorpion

Have you ever heard this fable?

One day, a scorpion set out on a journey through the forests and hills. He climbed over rocks and under vines and kept going until he reached a river. The river was wide and swift and he couldn't see any way to cross. So he ran upriver and then checked down river, all the while thinking that he might have to turn back.

Suddenly, he saw a frog sitting by the bank of the river. He decided to ask the frog for help getting across. "Hello Mr. Frog" called the scorpion, "Would you be so kind as to give me a ride on your back across the river?"

"Oh no, do you think I'm crazy?" said the frog. "We'll get half way across the river, you'll sting me and I'll drown. I'm not interested in drowning."

And the scorpion said, "You know, Frog, you're not thinking with that little bitty frog brain of yours. If I sting you half way across the river, it is true you will drown, but I would drown too. I'm not interested in drowning either."

This seemed to make sense to the frog so he agreed to take the scorpion across the river. The scorpion crawled onto the frog's back, his sharp claws prickling into the frog's soft hide, and the frog slid into the river. The muddy water swirled around them as the frog began swimming. Halfway across the river, the frog suddenly felt a sharp sting in his back and a deadening numbness began to creep into his body.

"You fool!" croaked the frog, "you stung me and now I'm going to drown. You are also going to drown. Why? Why on earth did you sting me?" The scorpion said, "I am a scorpion; scorpions sting." Then they both sank into the muddy waters of the swiftly flowing river.

How many scorpions do you know? I bet you know several. Scorpions attempt to pull you down with negativity and opposition. They can't get over their own weaknesses so they do whatever they can to stop your progress. They say things like, "We've always done it that way," or "That will never work" and even "That's a stupid idea." Scorpions will inject pain into your new dreams, goals, and ideas.

Some creatures and people just are what they are. It does not matter how nicely you treat them; their nature will cause them to sting you. You must be aware of scorpions in your life and stop giving them rides across the river. They are powerless until you decide to put them on your back. Ultimately, it's not the scorpion's fault you get swept away because you failed to recognize that scorpions sting. You knew what scorpions do and you chose to give them a ride across the river. If you do decide to give them a ride across the river, don't be surprised or complain when they sting you. After all, scorpions sting.

Waiting for Change

I'm waiting for change, just sitting here waiting for change. I'm waiting for a sunny day or a different job. I'm waiting for a new president. Yep — I'm just waiting for change. Once change happens, then I can really start living.

It's safe to say that change happens. The weather changes, careers change, and politics change. Walls have been knocked down and fences are being built. You can just sit there while everything changes around you, everything except what's important. Important things like your health, career, family, happiness, and success. Understand this basic life principle, in order for things to change for you, you must change. If you don't change yourself, the next five years of your life will look very similar to your last five.

The waiting for change mindset stinks. First, you wait until you graduate and then you wait around until you move to a place with more opportunity. You sit around and wait until you get married or have kids then life will really begin. Waiting for change sounds as foolish as working to retire. What's the point? If you're just waiting for change, you might as well go to the morgue and take a number. If you're just waiting for real life to begin, it never will.

Admit it, there will always be problems and challenges in your life. If you look hard enough, you can always find some unfinished business to be gotten through before real life begins. These problems and challenges are your life, and how you handle them determines your success. Are you going to wait for them to change or are you going to change them? To be successful, you can't wait for change.

Show some faith in yourself and take a chance. Rather than waiting for change, choose to create it. Start wherever you are right now and go after what you desire. Don't waste any more of your precious time. Use your energy, your thoughts and efforts to create change now. To succeed, you must grow where you're planted. Do what you can, where you are, with what you have. Everything will always be changing around you, but things won't change for you, not the important things unless you change them. You're life changes when you change.

Win-Win Mindset

Two sisters were fighting over the last orange in the fruit bowl. They went back and forth, each sister insisting that she should get it and both refusing to give up. Finally, one offers to split the orange down the middle and let each settle for half of what they truly wanted. To be sure it's fair, they decide that one will do the cutting and the other will get first choice of the two halves. They were about to cut the orange in half when their aunt walked in and realized what was going on. She turned to the girls and asked them each why they wanted the orange. As it turns out, one wanted to eat the orange, and the other wanted the peel to put in a cake. Once they realized this, they were able to "split" the orange in such a way that both got exactly what they wanted. They found the win-win solution.

It doesn't matter if you are negotiating for an orange, a house, or a multi-million dollar contract, the win-win mindset allows you to look for the solution that benefits all parties. Like the sisters, most people only care about WIIFM (what's in it for me). As a result, neither of them were going to get what they wanted. Never assume that the other party views the situation the same way you do, or you may create roadblocks over issues that are not relevant. When both sides learn about each other's objectives, there is a better chance of coming up with a solution that gets both of you what you want without either having to feel he or she lost.

The goal in negotiation should not be to win at the expense of someone else. Think about mutual gain, not just individual gain. By creating mutual gain, you maximize all parties' abilities to advance their purpose (eat the orange or make a cake). While your reasons may be different, the spirit behind your interests should be complementary. When you negotiate with a win-win mindset, you foster trust and allow all parties to walk away feeling like they won. Not all parties win all of the time, but the effort to get there builds a foundation for long-term successful relationships. When you strive for mutual advancement from the beginning, you build trust. If you start with and keep that win-win mindset, you can have your cake and eat the orange too.

Worry

The modern world provides many opportunities for worry. It's not usual to feel stressed out and overwhelmed. You worry about your family, your job, your health, your friends and your community. Worry is a lasting preoccupation with past or future events. There isn't one situation that is made better by worry. Worry has only one result — it makes matters worse. If you constantly worry, you'll never be able to focus on solutions.

Thinking through problems and challenges is a healthy response to life pressures and helps you to find solutions. Often, instead of logically thinking through problems, you get caught up with unresolved concerns and begin to worry. If not managed, worry quickly becomes an obstacle and you obsess over situations you can only partly control or are powerless to change. Worry will disrupt your life, hamper your ability to focus, and keep you from falling asleep at night.

No one is without problems; they are a part of living. Worry is a bad habit. The good news is, like any habit, it can be broken. Recognizing when you begin to worry is the beginning. Most people are unaware when they have started to worry. By being conscious of starting to worry, you can switch it off before it has the opportunity to affect your emotions and thoughts. You can reduce or eliminate worry by distracting your mind. Try thinking about something positive, going for a walk, splashing cold water on your face, calling a friend, or listening to your favorite music.

Stanley Allyn said, "There is no use worrying about things over which you have no control, and if you have control, you can do something about it instead of worrying." Don't get stressed out or overwhelmed. Worry solves nothing and only makes matters worse. If the cause of your worry is something you can change, then channel that worry into solutions. Don't focus on worry, focus on solutions.

AIDA Will Change Your Life

To get your message across, use the AIDA formula. It's simple, basic, and time-tested. AIDA has been around forever and is still being used today because it works! I was reminded again of its value at a seminar I just attended. It's easy to forget about and overlook when selling your products or ideas. The basic AIDA formula of getting Attention, creating Interest, arousing Desire, and producing Action is more relevant today than ever.

A - Attention

The typical consumer is bombarded with thousands of direct and subliminal messages; so getting attention is the most important and challenging part of this formula. Your message must excite consumers and hold their attention long enough to expose them to your brilliant ideas and great products. A great way of attracting attention is to offer something that sounds almost too outrageous to be true: "AIDA Will Change Your Life." If you can get their attention, you're well on your way.

I - Interest

Interest is developed by demonstrating the benefits of your ideas or products. Creating interest is answering the question your audience is subconsciously asking "What's in it for me?" Show them how their life will improve. People buy the benefits of the ideas and products that will enhance their lives, not the features. How does your offer positively affect their lives or solve their problems?

D - Desire

Arousing desire is all about ego. Convince people that your product or ideas will make things better — your products or ideas will make customer's lives easier and make them feel smarter and look younger. They buy because of ego, fear of loss, a guarantee, special bonus or price, not necessarily for logical reasons. That's basic human nature. And it's not about to change.

A - Action

If you have captured their attention, overwhelmed them with interest, and created an undeniable desire, you must ask them to take action. As the saying goes, "If you don't ask for it, you're never going to get it." You make the offer and ask them to take action. When you ask people to act, make it as easy as possible for them to do so. The easier it is for them to buy into your ideas or products, the better. Remember, sometimes you have to go a little further and "make them an offer they can't refuse."

Will AIDA change your life? I don't know about that, but that statement did get your attention. You showed at least enough interest to read this far. If you have enough desire, you might buy into the idea and take action. The basic AIDA formula is more relevant today than ever.

Ask Good Questions

Questions are powerful and guide you in your search for information. In order to coordinate your life, you need to know what other people are feeling and thinking. The answers to your questions open the door to knowledge and understanding. Asking good questions is the basis for effective communication.

Asking questions is very natural; asking *good* questions takes work. Poor questions will not help you find what you're looking for. Good questions allow you to get a grip on what is going on. Good questions lead to good information and the ability to put the picture together. Most people are not aware of the quality of questions they ask.

The quality of a question can be compared to casting a fishing line into someone's mind.

Poorly cast questions will bring in small fish; well cast questions will bring in big fish. Good questions are critical to effective communication and can help you discover solutions and inspire someone to take action.

Use the following four steps to ask good questions:

1. Think about and identify what kind of information you want to collect.

2. Work on one subject at a time. If you try to gather information about several subjects in one question, you probably won't get useful responses to any of them.

3. Listen. The most important part of a good question is listening. Probably no other aspect of communication is more ignored.

4. Ask follow up questions. The answer to the first question will give you the basis for follow-up questions.

Good questions are indispensable tools in the search for information and understanding. The answers to your good questions help you figure out what people are feeling and thinking. Effective communicators ask good questions.

Coffee and Doughnuts Anyone?

Stop the meeting madness!

I know you've been there, sitting through another mind-numbing meeting. It started late, you don't have a clue why you are there or what you're supposed to do. You can't wait until it's over — oh, look, coffee and doughnuts. Have you ever thought about how much money is actually being wasted at an unproductive meeting? Look around and add up the hourly value of the people zoned out around the conference table. Meetings are getting a bad rap for good reason — very little gets accomplished. The majority of meetings lack purpose, structure, and participation. Good news for you, besides the coffee and doughnuts, your meetings don't have to be that way.

Have you ever walked out of a meeting and immediately forgotten what it was about? This happens when meetings lack a purpose.

Always have a purpose and don't hide it in a power pointless presentation. Be very clear about why you are having the meeting, what is expected to be achieved during the meeting, and what needs to get done after the meeting. Hit the participants over the head with the purpose. Begin with the end in mind and think about the one big goal you'd like the meeting to accomplish. Be a cheerleader for the purpose.

What would you like everyone to think after the meeting? Everyone should leave knowing what the purpose was and what's expected of them. When the purpose is clear, people become passionate and creative.

To build structure into a meeting, set an agenda. Start on time and end on time. It helps all those involved to focus on what they are really trying to achieve and how best to reach that goal. Remember the opportunity costs: every minute a person spends in your meeting, is a minute they could be doing something else. A structure can show how meaningful the purpose is, and how well the team is working together.

Finally, a successful meeting contains effective communication. Healthy disagreement and debate are signs of passionate people and productive meetings. It is therefore crucial to get honest input from everyone. No one should feel afraid to say what they really think, and no one person or group should dominate the discussion. People must feel like their opinions are valued and taken seriously. Many people think a meeting is useful based on whether or not they were involved. When people participate, they take ownership and become responsible for outcomes.

How can you make sure your meetings are successful?

1. Have a Clear Purpose
   Hit them over the head with it.

2. Provide a Structure
   Stay on schedule using an agenda.

3. Gain Participation
   Get everyone involved.

These three points characterize a good meeting. A successful meeting doesn't come from coffee and doughnuts (or even pizza and beer). Productive, valuable, and engaging meetings require a clear purpose, structure and participation.

Confusion Is a Bad Strategy

Being clear is vital to success in any field of endeavor. Delivering a clear message in itself won't guarantee success; however, confusion will eventually lead to failure. Unless you are talking to Dionne Warwick's Psychic Friends Network, don't assume your audience understands you. To gain people's interest, agreement, and help, you must be as clear as possible. A confused mind will never say yes.

You confuse people when you throw as much material at them as possible hoping some of it "sticks". If you overwhelm them with information, they won't remember anything. Present your points in small chunks and sound bites. Make it easy for your audience to understand. Give them a little information and shut up. If they want more, they will ask.

Explicitly tell people right away what you're going to talk about. If your audience is wondering what your point is, they are confused. Remember the old saying, "Tell them what you're going to tell them," "tell them," and then "tell them what you told them." If you want them to take action, support your position, buy your service or product, approve your budget or proposal, tell them what they need to know. Don't leave them guessing.

When presenting, speak like you're talking to friends at the dinner table. Don't try to impress with big words or jargon. Using stories and metaphors helps people make sense of a crazy world and your message. The best speakers and leaders are masters at storytelling and metaphors.

People will forgive you for just about anything except being boring. Boredom certainly leads to confusion. If the audience is bored, they'll never get your message. It is difficult to get and keep an audience's attention. Attention spans are so short that we even have to abbreviate Attention Deficit Disorder. If you can't get your message across in eight minutes, or about the time between commercials during *Grey's Anatomy*, you've missed your opportunity.

Because a confused mind always says no. It is vital to be clear. Delivering a clear message in itself won't guarantee success, but it does get you on the right path. Don't overwhelm people with information. Get to the point, use stories and metaphors, and then shut up. Get your message across clearly because a confused mind will never say yes.

Crappy Co-worker

So, your co-worker has a crappy attitude . . .

"How do I deal with a co-worker who has a bad attitude?" is a question I'm asked often. A co-worker with a crappy attitude may make you miserable. There is no silver bullet that will turn their attitude from crappy to happy, but there are five steps you can take to stop their negative impact on your work environment. The five steps are: tell them, tell the boss, update your resume, tell the boss' boss, and finally, find a new place to work. This section covers step number one — tell them.

The first mistake people make when they have a co-worker with a crappy attitude is not saying anything. If you really want to change your work environment, you will have to deal with them head on. It will be difficult, but ignoring the problem will not solve it. The person with the crappy attitude needs to know that their behavior is not appreciated. It may not be your responsibility to change their attitude, but it is your responsibility to address the situation and tell the person.

Use the direct approach and say "Okay, your negative attitude is bringing me down and I would appreciate it if you'd stop." It is essential to voice your concerns. Don't let their continual crappy attitude curb your enthusiasm or you will get stuck in the muck. If you get stuck in the muck, you begin to develop a crappy attitude. Not telling them can lead to unpleasant consequences. If you have a co-worker with a crappy attitude, you have two choices: give up or do something about it. To do something about it, you must tell them.

If you went to your car after work and found that all of the air has been let out of your tires, what would you do? If you knew who did it, would you say anything to them? What would you do if they did it again the next day and then the day after that? They aren't really hurting you, they are just causing you a lot of frustration and anguish. While they are not causing you physical harm, I know you would say something to them. That co-worker with a crappy attitude is similar to the person letting the air out of your tires every day. While it does not appear to be a big deal or physically harm you, it is a huge pain in the butt and can cause you enough emotional stress that it will eventually affect you physically.

You have the potential and want to do a good job, but every day you battle crappy attitudes. Nothing sucks the life out of you faster, at work, than a co-worker's crappy attitude. These people deteriorate morale, lower productivity, and hurt the bottom line. If you do nothing and hope the situation will go away, it won't. Inaction will not correct the situation, only encourage it. You must refuse to tolerate bad attitudes and take the first step and tell your co-worker.

Tell Your Boss' Boss

Your company depends on you to do a good job and if something or someone is preventing you from doing a good job, your supervisors should know. If you have a co-worker with a crappy attitude, you have two choices, give up or do something about it. If you want to do something about it, follow these steps:

1. Tell your co-worker — they may not know they have a crappy attitude.

2. Tell your boss — crappy attitudes crush morale, lower productivity, and affect the bottom line.

3. Update your resume — this is a good idea, especially if you're making waves.

4. Tell your boss' boss — continue reading.

If you've told your direct supervisor and have seen no results, your next step is to tell the boss' boss. To change your environment, you must continue going up the chain of command. It is important because one person with a crappy attitude can have a negative impact on the entire company. Communicating with supervisors can be tricky. Remember, there is often more pressure on your supervisors than on you. Keep your cool and follow these workplace communication tips and you will be on your way to a better work environment.

1. Make an appointment — bosses have work to accomplish too.
2. Timing — when you ask can be almost as important as what you ask.
3. Be prepared — have written down talking points that accurately communicate the concerns.
4. Find common ground — find similar interests to help create unity and facilitates communication.
5. Smile — it makes communication smoother.
6. Eye contact — displays trust and confidence.
7. Body language — be aware that your body language makes up over half of the message.
8. Mirror your boss — use your boss' speaking tools (gestures, posture, vocabulary) for understanding.
9. Be clear — speak concisely and precisely.
10. Be patient — your supervisors must give employees a chance to correct their behavior.

Every day you communicate with many people: your significant other, your children, your friends, and the guy at the gas station, among others. However, your supervisors are people you communicate with that affect your work life significantly. If your supervisors are not aware you are unhappy, how can they help? Follow the steps to effectively communicate with someone who has direct control over you. Telling your boss' boss may not be easy, but it may be necessary to improve your workplace environment.

Get a New Job

You spend at least a third of your time at work. If you are miserable at work because of co-workers with crappy attitudes, you have two choices, give up or do something about it. If you want to do something about it, follow these steps:

1. Tell your co-worker — they may not know they have a crappy attitude.
2. Tell your boss – crappy attitudes crush morale and affect the bottom line.
3. Update your resume — this is a good idea, especially if you're making waves.
4. Tell your boss' boss — hope they are more helpful than your direct boss.
5. Get a new job — read on.

If you've followed the above steps with little or no success, you will eventually quit your job. It may not be today, this month, or this year. But it's inevitable. Face it, many of you have already quit your job — you just continue to go in and collect a paycheck. If you are miserable in your current job — one third of your life — it's time move on.

Many people daydream about leaving their jobs to find something more fulfilling, but they never do. Don't put it off one more day. Getting a new job will not be easy.

You may have heard — it's rough out there. Not only is unemployment high, but the situation doesn't seem to be getting better fast enough. Even though the job market may be brutal, the worst thing you can do is to continue going to work at a place you don't like. Not only will you not do your best work, it's like checking into a morgue each day.

Your job satisfaction, or lack thereof, is a huge factor in your life. If you don't like your job, you don't like a third of your life. Co-workers with crappy attitudes should not be tolerated. Bad feelings associated with your job rarely stay confined to the workplace. Those bad feelings spill over into your personal life and you'll begin to suffer from a kick-the-dog job. (A job that makes you want to kick your dog.) Typically, it's not so much the job that is the problem, it's the people associated with the job.

If you have a co-worker with a crappy attitude, and you've found it difficult, if not impossible, to solve, you need to get a new job. You need to look out for your best interests. Your job consumes too many hours of too many days of your life for you to stay in it if you're miserable. No excuses. If you have a co-worker with a crappy attitude and you can't fix it, get a new job.

Get an Edge

"According to most studies, people's number one fear is public speaking. Number two is death. Death is number two. Does that sound right? This means to the average person, if you go to a funeral, you're better off in the casket than doing the eulogy." Jerry Seinfeld

Because the majority of people fear public speaking and try to avoid it at any cost, being able to speak in public gives you an edge. Public speaking — from presenting a report to a small team to making a big pitch before a packed room of potential investors — gives you an edge seldom achieved by excellent work alone.

Speaking in public creates opportunities. Public speaking increases your exposure and develops credibility, knowledge, and expertise. Speaking in front of others is the easiest way to increase your group of friends and sphere of influence. The more you practice speaking, the better you will get. Soon, you'll be invited to speak and share your knowledge to audiences full of people that can hire you and/or buy your products. Businesses and organizations understand communicating ideas in public is a rare ability and are always on the look out for those who can effectively do it. Instead of dreading public speaking, treat it as an opportunity.

I'm sure you are smart and talented. I'm sure you have great skills and ideas. There are two possible outcomes if you fear public speaking and can't share your ideas. You either don't share your ideas or someone else shares them for you and gets the credit. The people who are succeeding are not necessarily those who are smarter or know more, it is often those who can speak in public. If you intend to be heard and make a meaningful difference, you must be able to speak well in public.

Being able to speak in public is one of life's competitive advantages. It moves you up to a different league. You can get this competitive advantage because the serious business of public speaking is a learned skill and not as difficult as people make it seem. You're not performing brain surgery. People don't expect you to be perfect, just personable. You'll need the courage to begin improving by signing up for a class, getting a coach or mentor, reading a book, or watching a DVD. You will also need the right attitude.

Imagine all the benefits of public speaking. How would your life be different if you embraced public speaking as an opportunity rather than fearing it? Speaking in public gives you an edge. OK, maybe people would rather read the eulogy than be in the casket, but most of them would much rather be in the back of the room than in the front. Being able to speak in public gives you many strong advantages; gain the skill and use it.

In the Flow

Have you ever been so fully absorbed in an activity that you lost track of time, your self-consciousness fell away, and you felt like you could accomplish activities effortlessly? Being in the flow (or in the zone — as many athletes call it) is that place mentally and physically where everything is going perfectly for you. You feel as if you can finish any project, run twenty miles, make any shot, sink any putt, or call anyone. That feeling of being totally immersed in what you are doing is not reserved for the Michael Jordans, Lance Armstrongs, or Tiger Woods of the world. You too can get in the flow. By consciously creating opportunities to get in the flow, you infuse each day with a heightened sense of accomplishment and satisfaction.

Getting in the flow may be elusive at times and takes work to achieve. Total immersion has identifiable characteristics. By understanding the characteristics, it is possible to influence your performance in a way that increases the likelihood of achieving flow.

Raise your awareness and create conditions conducive to getting in the flow over and over again.

A few identifiable characteristics of *being in the flow* are:

- Clear Goals
- Focus
- Lack of Ego
- Timelessness
- Control
- Reward

Awareness of these characteristics allows you to find that magical place where your mind and the activities you do work in perfect synch. In the flow, you are completely focused and motivated. Working in the flow helps you channel your emotions and actions towards the activity at hand and your highly focused state of consciousness allows you to work at the peak of your abilities.

Multitasking

You've heard that multitasking comes with a steep price tag. If you want to be really productive, you should focus on one task rather than a bunch of them. Heck, you're probably multitasking right now. Are you checking your e-mail, using your phone, or watching TV? Common sense tells you that the quality of your work deteriorates as you keep more balls in the air. You know that your performance is better if you focus entirely on one ball at a time. Why do you do it then? Multitasking has become a normal way of functioning in the world.

Many people define multitasking as juggling, which begs the question, do you even know how to juggle? Multitasking without knowing how to juggle will inevitably lead to dropping some balls. The interesting thing is that the human mind is so amazing; it allows you to appear as though you can comfortably perform this juggling act. You believe you can e-mail, drive, talk on the phone, write a proposal and watch *Grey's Anatomy* at the same time. While you may appear successful at multitasking, the more you juggle the less efficient you become at performing any one task.

I'm not going to tell you not to multitask. That would be foolish and a waste of time.

Think about it, when was the last time you did just one thing for a half-hour? The key is to be aware that you are multitasking and understand that as good as you think you are at multitasking, your overall performance goes down. The best multitaskers recognize when to juggle and when to play catch. You wouldn't play catch with three balls, would you? If the task is important, work on that task until completion. The best multitaskers recognize important tasks and focus 100% of their energy on that single task until completed.

Rather than helping you, multitasking can actually increase your stress because you try to hold more information in your memory than is effectively possible. This can give you the feeling of being disorganized and can cause mistakes. The simple solution is to avoid multitasking altogether. However, that's not very practical in the world in which you live. You can juggle multiple tasks at once, just be aware that your brain is limited. With each new task you toss into the air, your performance goes down. Know the difference between the times you can juggle many balls in the air and the times you must play catch and focus on one.

Music of the Moment

(Inspired by my mentor and friend Douglas A. Cox)

Imagine a huge ballroom with a great big empty hardwood dance floor. Hanging from the ceiling is one of those cool, mirrored, spinning, lighted balls. You're at one end of the room and the person you want to talk to is way at the other end. Can you see all the space between?

Can you hear the music? From today forward, when you communicate with someone, think of it as sharing a song with someone. Get on the same emotional level and ask them to verbally dance. Share a moment in time on that big communication dance floor. A secret to effective communication is listening for the music of the moment.

It is the music of conversations that moves lives. Listen to the music. Become aware of the situation and conditions around you. Before you go swinging on to the dance floor, first pay attention to the song. Can you swing to it? Or is it more of headbanger song? If you're hearing Harry Connick, Jr., and the person you're communicating with hears Metallica, it's going to be an ugly dance.

Being aware of the music before you open your mouth changes your approach and improves communication skills. You begin to take responsibility for the success of the conversation. It's only then that you can truly perform the right moves. Be flexible, adjust your style to fit the music of the moment, and always be prepared for a change of songs.

Think about the rhythm of your spouse after a long day. Check the tempo of your kids or co-workers when you first see them. Before you talk, listen for the music. Check the situation around you. Is it *"Hot In Here"* or like *"Ice, Ice, Baby"*? Are you talking to a *"Dancing Queen"* or girls that *"Just Want To Have Fun"*? Is the dance floor full of people in *"Celebration"* or is it *"Unforgettable"*? The answers determine whether you should *"Get The Party Started"* or show a little *"Respect."*

Verbally dance. Get on the same emotional level and share a moment in time under the spinning light in the middle of that communication dance floor. For effective communication in your personal and professional life, hear the song and listen for the music of the moment.

PowerPointLess Presentation

The "PowerPointLess Presentation" — you know the drill, you're confined in a dimly lit room and expected to absorb material from a large screen with the help of a laser beam. No amount of coffee, Diet Pepsi, or Red Bull can keep you focused. Nothing bores an audience faster than a presenter flipping through one endless slide after another.

PowerPoint is a great support tool and, unfortunately, its misuse leads to boredom and confusion.

The engineers at Microsoft envisioned a program that would help people communicate more effectively and efficiently. They didn't know that they were creating a program that people would misuse, making communication less effective. A PowerPoint presentation should be used as a visual aid to clarify your message not as the presentation itself.

For many people, PowerPoint is a crutch. Day after day people stand up and read the information from slides, throwing out as much information as possible in the allotted time in the hopes that something sticks. Don't expect anyone to understand the power of your point if you have 47 bullets flying across the screen to music. All the bells and whistles of a "PowerPointLess" presentation end up boring and confusing your audience.

Many people hide behind the security of PowerPoint slides and end up being completely detached from the information they are presenting and the audience. Reading from the slides verbatim insults your audience. Do you really think people can't read what is on the screen? The audience has come to see a presentation, not a slide show. If all you're going to do is read information off of a slide, e-mail it to them instead and let them read it on their own time.

If you dislike sitting through "PowerPointLess" presentations, why, when it's your turn, do you present the same way? Misuse of PowerPoint reduces your effectiveness. PowerPoint is an excellent support tool but should not be the presentation. PowerPoint will never turn a bad presentation into a good one, and it will not convert an ineffective presenter into an effective one. If your message is confusing, words and images flying across the screen and blowing up will not help. The newest computers and latest programs simply magnify the oldest problem in human relations, delivering a clear message.

You Are Not the Boss of Me

Who is the boss of you?

If you produce an output and get paid for it, you are the boss of you. Even if you work for someone else, you are self-employed, and like it or not, you own a business. It makes no difference who signs the front and who signs the back of your paycheck. You are a company of one in the business of selling your output for profit. Be the boss of you and take complete responsibility for your company's failures and success.

Do not operate under the assumption that your customer (maybe the company you work for) will magically continue to provide you with a paycheck every two weeks. When you consider yourself self-employed, it becomes very obvious that what you do has a direct impact on the results. You can attempt to blame your failures on someone else, but in the end, you're accountable for yourself and will always be stuck with full responsibility. When you're in charge, you can decide what you want out of life.

As the boss of a one-employee company, you are accountable for every facet of the business. The boss is in charge of promotion, sales, production, quality control, personal development, communication, and the bottom line. Do not be willing to leave these important responsibilities to someone else. You determine the value of your company. You can no longer make excuses; you must make progress.

If you produce an output and get paid for it, even if you work for someone else, you should really think like the boss of your own company. When you do, you become responsible and accountable for every part of your company. You may have to suspend or fire yourself from time to time for poor performance. Don't worry; you can always hire yourself back. You are a company of one in the business of selling your output for profit. Who's the boss of you?

Actions Are Words in Motion

Watch your thoughts; they become words. Watch your words; they become actions. Frank Outlaw

There's a powerful connection between the words you use and the resulting actions. Your thoughts paint the pictures and your words turn those pictures to actions. When you are determined that something is going to happen, you talk about it. When you talk about something enough (good or bad), it happens.

The words that you use to describe what is happening around you trigger emotions of happiness or unhappiness. When you talk about things positively, your experiences are positive. When you talk about things negatively, your experiences are (big surprise) negative.

Think about the last time you saw a really well-behaved dog. Listen to the words its master uses. I bet you heard words of encouragement similar to "you're such a good dog" and "you're the best dog ever." Dogs that consistently hear good words take positive actions. Dogs that are yelled at all of the time are usually not great dogs. It's the same principle with children. I know the cutest, smartest, most well-behaved one-year-old girl ever. It is not a coincidence that her mom tells her how cute, how smart, and how well behaved she is many times each day. You see, actions are often words in motion.

Make the decision to change your attitude and then words and your actions will follow. When your actions change, the resulting experiences change. A single and simple act such as changing the way you speak, or changing your wording makes all the difference. It's like throwing a pebble into a pond; you see a splash and hear the plunk of the pebble. You notice the rippling circles moving out from where the pebble hit the water. That ripple effect can literally transform your world.

The starting point of becoming a more positive person is to monitor and control your words. The quality of your experiences are determined by your actions. Your actions from moment to moment are determined by the words you speak. If you control your words, you can literally talk yourself into the experiences you choose. You make decisions constantly, decisions that powerfully affect your life. Make the decision now to control your words and you've made the decision to determine your experiences. Actions are words in motion.

Active Listening

Grandma said, active listening is a habit and essential for effective communication. When you actively listen, it shows you are wise and builds the faith that others have in you. Active listening is the process of listening and responding to another person that improves mutual understanding. I always think about what Grandma said when I was a kid, "Matthew — you've got two ears and one mouth. Listen twice as much as you talk."

Many people consider listening as simply not talking. Active listening is much more than just not talking; it is being mentally engaged in what the other person is saying. You build a connection that goes beyond words. It is through active listening that people connect and develop trust and rapport. Active listening strengthens your relationships.

Listen actively to break down barriers and communication becomes easier. Active listening can minimize conflicts and misunderstandings. To do this, you must focus on the speaker in order to better understand the message. Often when others are talking, people don't listen at all. They are distracted, half listening, and half thinking about picking the kids up from soccer or what to mix with the Hamburger Helper. If you are a poor listener, your productivity will suffer simply because you do not have the tools needed to influence, persuade, and negotiate. To perform to expectations and succeed, you must be able to actively listen.

If you're finding it particularly difficult to concentrate on what someone is saying, try repeating their words mentally after they say them. This will reinforce their message and help you control mind drift. To enhance your listening try to:

- Focus on the Speaker
- Ask Questions
- Be Non-judgmental
- Paraphrase
- Empathize
- Squarely Face the Speaker
- Open Your Posture
- Lean Towards the Speaker
- Maintain Eye Contact
- Relax

Active listening takes time and practice and does not produce results overnight. When you practice active listening, your conversations will get easier, not just for you, but also for the speaker. As an excellent communicator, you must lead the way. Remember what Grandma said, "You've got two ears and one mouth — listen twice as much as you talk."

Breathe, Then Smile

Smiling is the ultimate positive gesture. It is a universal language and is almost never misunderstood. A smile, regardless of your age, culture, ethnicity, financial status, faith, or nationality, shows you are genuine and builds a connection. Next to breathing, a smile is the most important thing you can do.

Smiling is the currency that can buy you anything. A smile will buy you a job at the interview, a sale while on the job, excellent service, and even love. It's simple, effective, and the quickest way to be perceived as more likable, friendly, warm, and approachable. A smile puts people at ease and generates positive feelings about you professionally and personally. A smile is so powerful it has been known to break ice.

There are as many different types of smiles as there are people. There are bashful smiles, embarrassed smiles, goofy smiles, thoughtful smiles, bold smiles, gentle smiles, toothy smiles, "*I love you*" smiles, smiles of gratitude, and smiles of agreement. A smile is the number one form of nonverbal communication. It's your welcome sign; it's a hug, handshake, or high five from a distance. A smile radiates warmth that draws others to you. It's what makes you attractive.

Some people naturally have a great smile; others must work at it. To increase your smile currency, you must first become aware of smiling. Take notice of others around you. Look at people you admire. Are their smiles warm and inviting? Do they smile with their whole face or just their mouth? Be aware of your own smile. Are you projecting the image you want? Do you look genuine? Are you building a connection?

Smiling involves muscles, and just like other muscles, to make them bigger and stronger, you must exercise them. Find a mirror or look at some recent pictures. If you don't like your smile, you need to practice. Work on expressing your smile with your lips, your eyes, and your heart. No matter what shape, size, or strength, the more you smile, the more it becomes natural (kind of like breathing). Smiling often can change everything in your life for the better.

Smiling is a universal language. It shows you are genuine and builds a connection. When it comes to communicating effectively, smiles are nothing less than pure absolute magic. Remember, breathe first, then smile.

Do You No?

We have the power to choose our attitudes. Why then, do people choose to be negative? I believe it is because of conditioning. A UCLA study reported that the average one-year-old hears the word "no" more than 400 times per day! It is one of the first words we hear and one of the first words we learn. By the age of 18, we've heard the word no over 200,000 times, compared to just a few thousand yes messages. We'll continue to hear negative words like no over and over again for the rest of our lives.

For safety reasons, it is good to understand no early on in life, but hearing no on a continual basis is detrimental. We end up learning much of what to do by being told what not to do. The human brain does not efficiently process negative commands or statements. If I tell you, for example, "not to spill the glass of milk", you have to actually think about spilling the glass of milk so you can take the required steps to not spill the milk. If I tell you "not to think about a pink elephant", you have to actually think about a pink elephant to take the steps to not think about a pink elephant. Unfortunately, what you focus on becomes your reality. By telling you not to spill the glass of milk or not to think about a pink elephant, you may end up spilling the glass of milk all over the pink elephant.

Words condition our thoughts. Negative words are gloomy, harsh, and imply wrongdoing. They deny, refuse, and disagree instead of offering suggestions or alternatives. The constant bombardment of negative words can tear us down. It is always more positive to ask for what you want rather than what you don't want. But how do you know what you want? Is it more clear to you what you don't want? How's that for confusing?

It is true that we have the power to choose our attitudes, and it is no surprise that most people have been conditioned to be negative. Throw yourself a curve ball. Try choosing to be positive. "I like Mondays." "I am going to enjoy my visit with my mother-in-law." By choosing the positive words, your mind will take the necessary steps to achieve the positive. If by chance, you do spill your glass of milk on a pink elephant, you can choose not to cry about it.

See page 98, for a discussion on ways that No should be used correctly to improve your life.

Gossip Gone Wild

Have you been the victim of gossip? Have you been one to gossip? Listen around — gossip has gone wild. Gossip is a major pastime and the mainstay of companies, organizations, and the media. Talking behind someone's back isn't just part of a conversation, it has become the conversation. Don't deny it; we've all participated in it and sometimes even relished it. Gossip is a time-consuming destructive behavior. Minimize the gossip in your life and your life will automatically be more positive.

The biggest gossipers are always those people with the lowest self esteem. What better way to improve your own image than by talking behind someone's back. Do you think so little of yourself that the only way to feel good is to tear others down? If talking behind someone's back displays poor self esteem, so does listening to it. Thus the bombardment of recycled rumors, catty appraisals, backhanded compliments, and sarcasm continues.

Gossip spreads in a flash and spawns distrust. It ruins reputations — not just the subject of the gossip, but the gossiper's reputation too. Every time you gossip, it is a reflection of your insecurities. You may think it is simply talking about other people, but in reality gossiping is all about you. When you speak negatively about someone, the listener often attributes those same traits to you the speaker. In other words, if you gossip about someone cheating, the person listening may well perceive you as dishonest.

If gossip has gone wild around you, try these simple techniques to minimize the impact:

• When gossip starts, change the subject.
• Build people up. Do not tear them down.
• Challenge the facts.
• If gossip persists, walk away.

When you participate in gossip, you damage your credibility and create a negative environment. Instead, try keeping your mouth closed, or changing the subject, or even walking away. The effect of minimizing the gossip in your life is uplifting and refreshing.

You'll find smoother communications, enhanced team-work, and improved overall productivity.

Participating in gossip only gives fuel to another conver-sation down the road without you and about you. I chal-lenge you to minimize your gossip and focus on more positive conversations.

Participation

Think of a time when a message really stuck in your head. Was it a memorable experience? I bet the presentation involved participation. Participation is a key element in the communication process. Do not underestimate the value of participation, because it actively engages the learner and aids retention of the message.

To improve upon your communication skills, incorporate participation into your speeches and presentations. Participation connects the speaker and audience, creating a memorable experience. Highly engaged audiences feel respected, valued, and take ownership of the information. They become responsible for their own learning. Learning is, by nature, an act of participation.

Building participation into speeches and presentations takes extra effort, and audiences don't always like to cooperate. Your extra effort will be rewarded. Encourage participation with a variety of activities and techniques. Simple ideas include playing music, using flip charts, and Post-It notes. Have people work in pairs or small groups, ask open-ended questions, utilize role playing and storytelling. Think about turning your presentations into Broadway shows with theatrical techniques, props, and costumes. Participation makes the experience much more memorable.

You will also increase participation by limiting the use of PowerPoint. PowerPoint is a great support tool, and unfortunately, the most abused. Reading the text from a slide does nothing to involve your audience. In fact, it decreases participation. Text on a PowerPoint slide does nothing to involve your audience.

A successful speech or presentation is the result of careful planning, preparation, and practice. Effective communicators use a blend of content and audience participation to create a program that involves and informs. For the most part, audiences want to be engaged in a memorable experience and retain the message. Meaningful participation is a key element. Do not underestimate the value.

Power of the Pause

"I think, therefore I am." (Rene Descartes, 1637)

"I pause, therefore I think." (Matt Booth, 2005)

"A picture paints a thousand words." (Chinese proverb)

"A pause paints a thousand pictures." (Matt Booth, 2004)

The power of the pause is nothing short of amazing. A pause when talking accomplishes three major tasks: it replaces filler words; lets your audience paint a picture; and allows you, the speaker, to think on your feet. Your communication effectiveness will improve if you work consciously on using the power of the pause.

Uttering useless sounds to cover uncomfortable moments of silence is one of the worst habits people can acquire when it comes to expressing themselves. Have you ever found yourself counting the "ums" and "uhs" in a presentation? Have you ever counted your own? Filler words dilute the value of your message and rob your speech of strength, making you appear unsure or tentative. The remedy for filler words is the pause. The pause allows your mind to catch up with your mouth and prevents you from saying "um" and "uh" fifty-seven times.

The power of the pause allows the minds of your audience to catch up with your mouth as well. In speaking, the pause is equivalent to the paragraph in the written word.

Paragraphs set apart one idea from the next and give the reader some white space to reflect.

Pausing when you talk gives the audience white space. Pausing for two or three seconds at the end of a phrase or sentence will feel like an eternity to you and will be bliss to your listeners.

Audiences require regular and numerous pauses to paint a picture in their mind. People don't remember what you say; they remember the picture they see in their minds. An old Chinese proverb states "A picture paints a thousand words." If a picture paints a thousand words, a pause paints a thousand pictures.

You've also heard the phrase, "I think, therefore I am." I often tell people, "I pause, therefore I think." Imagine you are speaking to a large audience. Your mind goes blank, you can't remember what you've said and you don't know what to say next. What do you do? You ramble, spit out some filler words, and try to hide behind the projection screen. Next time you lose track of where you are, don't fill your presentation with "you knows" and "rights." Simply pause, look at the audience as if you had planned to stop at this point, THINK, and start again. You paused, therefore you thought.

The power of the pause will not go unnoticed. Be aware of your filler words when they sneak into casual conversations and formal presentations. The pause is your pal. It replaces filler words, lets your audience paint a picture, and allows you to think on your feet. Your communication effectiveness will improve if you work consciously to add the POWER of the PAUSE to your arsenal.

Storytelling

Human beings have been communicating with each other through storytelling since we lived in caves and sat around fires. In a time when technology seems to be taking over the world, don't underestimate the value of the ancient art of storytelling. Storytelling is the original and most powerful form of communication. When a story is told, a connection is formed and information and ideas are better understood. Everyone loves stories and has one to tell. What's your story?

Everyone has a story; in fact, they have hundreds of them. We learn how to tell stories at a very young age. Stories help us make sense of a chaotic world and validate us as humans. The ability to tell a good story often determines your success. Stories reveal whether you can be trusted; they separate you from your competition and bond you with your audience.

Storytelling maximizes the connection between you and your listeners by encouraging them to imaginatively recreate their own story. Stories capture and hold attention. Stories can make a point, teach a lesson, or sell a product or service. Stories can be used one-on-one, in small groups, or in front of thousands of people.

People remember stories and rapidly absorb the information and ideas presented. Good communication is developed through logic, but facts and figures alone result in the eyes glazing over and PowerPoint burnout. Stories have the capability to translate dry, abstract numbers into compelling pictures. A grand story is full of emotions and feelings.

Your audience can't begin to remember everything you say, but they will remember how your stories made them feel.

For the caveman, the world was a strange and unexplained place. Storytelling was used to make sense of the world. In a time when technology seems to be taking over, the world can again be strange and unexplained. You are bombarded with information and the clutter of countless choices. Stories cut through that clutter and help you make sense of the world. Stories shape your life. Storytelling enables you to tell stories, especially to tell your story.

What's your story?

Talking

Many misunderstandings in today's world are a direct result of failed communications. Unclear communication leads to confusion and failed events. Talking is a major player in the communication process; unfortunately, most people put little thought into talking and end up rambling too fast without making a point. When it's your time to talk, proceed slowly, be clear and concise.

Communication is the exchange of information and ideas. It is sending an image from one person's mind to another. As simple as that sounds, it is one of the most complicated tasks humans ever do. Communicating a clear message is hard work. Contrary to popular belief, it is not a natural process and requires learning and practice. You succeed when the receiver understands the image you intended to send.

If I say the word *frog*, what image pops into your mind? Do you see the letters F-R-O-G or do you see the picture of a FROG? What type of frog do you see? Is it an enormous ugly bullfrog or Kermit the Frog? Effective communication happens when everyone see the same frog. When you talk, by speaking slowly in a clear and concise manner, you increase the chance that your audience will see the same frog as you.

Begin by slowing down. Most people get excited and simply talk too fast. Use short, simple sentences and common words. It's tough to understand someone who speaks fast and runs words together. Talking fast muddies and reduces the importance of your message, giving your audience a license to daydream.

Fast talking feeds another problem, rambling. Rambling, or beating around the bush, is jumping from thought to thought, using more words than necessary and failing to make a point. Don't do it. Use simple words and use only enough of them to get your point across.

Be aware of how you talk. Are you talking too fast? Is your message clear or muddied? Maybe you ramble on and on without ever making a point? How you talk shapes your thoughts, your actions and the way others see you. Slowing down, being clear, and reducing the number of words used enhances your communication effectiveness. When it's your time to talk, make the most of it and let your audience see the same frog.

The Value of No

No is a priceless word in your vocabulary. This little word adds big value to your life when used correctly.

Saying no will help you be more productive and reduce stress. No sets limits about what you will or will not do. It allows you to focus on the things you say yes to.

Life is full of demands and opportunities. If you constantly say yes to the demands of your life, you forfeit some of the opportunities of your life. You'll glumly spend your time helping others accomplish their agendas. Learning to say no is one of the biggest favors you can do for yourself. That little word can free you from burdens. There are times when you simply have too much going on to say yes and stay productive. Even if you think you can, you really can't do it all. In order to stay focused on your agenda, rather than someone else's, say no. If you say yes to everything that is asked of you, you will burn out. The use of no increases the value of your yeses.

Don't confuse rejection of a request with rejection of the person making the request. Saying no doesn't mean you don't like the person; you're just refusing their current request. The phrase "I'll try to be there" in response to a party invitation is giving yourself an excuse to avoid a commitment. It doesn't do anyone any favors. Others depend on your no just as they do your yes. Answering with a maybe is inconsiderate.

You have the right to say no. No is not a dirty or selfish word. Be polite, be firm and say no. Don't raise your voice or become upset, simply say that you cannot help this time.

When you say no, say it straightforwardly and with confidence. When you say no to a request, you are creating space to say yes to something else. To remain in control of your time and life and minimize stress, you must say no It can be hard, and you may feel badly about it, but in the end you'll be happier, you'll get more done, and the people you live and work with will actually be better off for it as well. You'll find it easier to say no if you:

- Realize the value of your time.
- Know your priorities.
- Have and review written goals.
- Practice saying no.
- Don't apologize for saying no.
- Stop being so gosh darn nice.

No is a priceless word in your vocabulary and adds big value to your life. Learning to say no will reduce stress and help you be more productive. Each time you say yes to a demand in your life, you are saying no to an opportunity in your life. Be happy and get yourself a long list of nos and focus on a short list of yeses. Check out page 85 for a discussion on the detrimental effect the overuse of no.

The Voice

Your lips are moving but all I hear is "blah, blah, blah." The voice is a vital communication tool that is often overlooked. People go an entire day, week, month, year, and even lifetime without ever thinking about their voice. In fact, the only time we think about our voice is when we lose it. As long as sound comes out when you move your lips, everything is OK. Whether you think about it or not, how you sound shapes how people perceive you and that perception is important to your overall success.

You know the old saying, "It's not what you say — it's how you say it." The actual meaning of the words you use account for a small percentage of the communication process. You can spend entirely too much time thinking about the words to say and not enough time thinking about how you say them. To improve your speaking voice and maximize its power, be aware of these five vocal components. They are tone, pitch, volume, pace, and melody. By thinking about each one, you will realize there is much more to speaking than merely moving your lips.

Tone is the edgy sound in your voice. It reflects emotion and mood. The tone of your voice carries social information such as authority and humor.

The pitch refers to the highness or lowness of your voice. Pitch which is too high can be quite irritating to listeners. It is important to vary your pitch to add inflection to your voice. Think of Mike Tyson versus James Earl Jones. Who would you rather listen to?

Volume is how soft or loud you speak. Most people speak too softly when addressing others. An effective voice fills a room with a strong sound that commands attention without shouting. You should vary the volume you use with certain words or phrases to add emphasis to your message.

Pace is how slow or fast you speak. Do you speak fast like a slick salesperson whom nobody can trust, or a bit too slowly, forcing the other person to question your intelligence?

Melody is the way your voice moves up and down in a particular musical pattern. It can turn your voice into an instrument. When you lack melody, you come across as monotone and boring.

Being aware of these five vocal components gives you an advantage over others, because most people never think about their voice unless it's gone. This awareness creates change. Whether you like it or not, people will make judgments about you solely based on the way you sound. With a little practice, your voice will be a powerful communication tool that grabs attention. So when your lips are moving, people will hear something other than "blah, blah, blah."

Thoughts Determine Words

Your thoughts determine your words. What you spend most of your time thinking about is what you spend most of your time talking about. What you talk about turns into the events you experience. Your successes (or lack of them) are results of your thinking. Your thinking today produces your words today and your words become your actions.

Realizing the powerful connection between your thoughts and words is one of the most important lessons you can learn. Thoughts determine words.

Words come from thoughts. If you never thought something, you would never say it. It is simple, think good thoughts and speak good words. Think bad thoughts and speak bad words. Your words are products of your mind and your success depends on the nature and quality of those products. Whether you think it will be a good day or a bad day, you're probably right. If you think Mondays suck and Fridays are great, you are rarely disappointed. The difference between Mondays and Fridays is the six inches between your ears.

If you are consumed by negative thinking and speaking, do everything you can to squeeze positive thoughts into your mind. It will not come naturally or easily at first. Being aware of negative thoughts allows you to replace them with positive thoughts. You will always be tempted to think negatively but don't give in to temptation. Recognize the powerful connection between your thoughts and words. What you think about the majority of the time is your choice. You control your thoughts which determine your words. Watch your thoughts carefully for they become your words. As you change your thoughts, your words will change and so will your actions!

Um Disease

Uttering useless filler words to cover up moments of silence is one of the worst diseases a person can catch. Um Disease, as it is called, is when a person uses too many filler words during the communication process. Filler words have no meaning and have, unfortunately, become part of everyday conversation. Examples of filler words include; "um," "ah," "like," "basically," and "you know." Um Disease is an epidemic that, left untreated, can lead to a severe communication crisis. It is a chronic stumbling block that prevents millions of people from delivering a clear message.

Um Disease begins when one contagious "um" leads to a series of "ums" and "ahs." It keeps you from getting your point across quickly and clearly. Because the early stages cause little or no pain, most people who have Um Disease don't even realize it. Even in its mildest form, Um Disease is an indicator of poor communication skills and should be treated immediately.

In moderate cases, the listener's attention is lost and mind drift occurs. Um Disease gives the impression that the speaker is unsure and tentative. As the condition advances, the listeners' ears may redden, swell, and even bleed. With time, one "um" will spread and multiply into many filler words. Often, this destructive disease is over-looked and leads to confusing messages and ruined credibility.

Um Disease is hard to avoid. Unlike many diseases that are only caught on vacation or in public bathroom stalls, Um Disease can be found everywhere. Filler words dilute the value of your message and rob your speech of strength and clarity. The continual use of filler word is a warning sign of Um Disease. If caught in the early stages, it can be corrected with treatment. Advance cases of Um Disease require professional help — take a class, join a speakers' organization, or get a speech coach.

Healthy speech is free of filler words. To cure Um Disease, you must first be aware you are infected. If you don't remove filler words from your conversation, you run the risk of Um Disease spreading and damaging the clarity of your entire message.

Be Yourself

When you were a kid, what did you want to be when you grew up? Can you even remember? Did you want to be a doctor, policeman, fireman, teacher, or even president? As a kid, you could be yourself and dream about anything. In real terms, being yourself means identifying your uniqueness and using it to serve others.

Every person has unique talents and the ability to develop them. Unfortunately, many people never discover, or fail to develop, their talents. Numerous people live their entire lives never doing what they are good at. They never get to be the person they wanted to be when they grew up.

Being yourself is not a nice-to-have quality; it's imperative. You should work harder on developing yourself than you do on your job. You spend a great deal of time and energy earning paychecks. How much time and energy do you invest on developing yourself?

I encourage you to be yourself. It is the only way to be happy. It is tiring and useless trying to be someone else. It is hard work trying to fool people everyday into thinking you are someone else. It is not effective or productive to try and be someone you are not. Free yourself from what others think and work on developing yourself.

Discover or rediscover your unique talents, develop them,

d use them to serve others. Make the commitment ght now to be yourself. It is the only way to be truly happy. Become what you wanted to be as a kid. Be outstanding at being yourself. Focus your energy on being yourself and you will be happy and successful. The amazing part is, when you do this, it is as if you cannot fail.

Blame Game

Who did you blame today? Did you point your finger at your boss, coworkers, significant other, kids, or parents? Someone else is surely to blame for whatever went wrong. The only thing better than blaming others by yourself is when you can get together with a group of like-minded blamers and agree on one thing; it is someone else's fault. This victim mind-set, finger pointing, and lack of personal responsibility is widespread, just take a listen. The blame game kills opportunity for personal growth.

Everyone screws up. If you don't screw-up, check the obituaries because you're dead.

Unfortunately, it's now the norm to deny responsibility and blame others. If I go out and drink a 12–pack of Bud Light and make a fool myself on the town plaza, who should I blame? I could put the blame on my parents, an ex-girlfriend, my buddies, or maybe even the bartenders? Out of all the beer I've drunk in my life, I can't remember someone ever forcing one down my throat. Everything in my life is a result of the choices I make.

Taking responsibility for my screw-ups means I admit it, apologize to everyone I've offended (that I can remember), try to learn something, forgive myself, and move on.

We all screw-up and it's very convenient to deny responsibility and blame others. After all, it couldn't possibly be my fault for missing an appointment. I know it's not your fault your job sucks or your house is a mess. I know you didn't mean to smoke that pack of cigarettes, besides, you only smoke when you're drinking. Being overweight is not your fault either; you just don't have time to exercise and you accidentally ate that box of doughnuts. Taking responsibility for your screw-ups (no matter how big or small) allows you to learn something from them, then get over them. The blame game kills any opportunity for growth. But I am sure it is not your fault.

Build Emotional Muscle

Think back to a time you started a new exercise program. It was hard at first, and you had aches and pains in places you didn't even know you had muscles. When you pushed too hard, you may have even been in considerable discomfort. This happens because you were using your muscles in new or in different ways. You were trying to create physical change and initially received physical discomfort. Just as you build muscle in your body, you must build muscle in your mind. When you exercise your mind, you build emotional muscle.

When you're in a discomfort zone, you must decide if you are willing to go through the pain until you've adjusted. That decision determines whether the goal is met and muscle is built. The same thing happens when building emotional muscle. When you exercise your mind in new and different ways, you will have emotional pain. You must decide if you are willing to go through the emotional discomfort to build that emotional muscle.

To take on new challenges, you must build up physical and emotional strength and endurance. Approach new challenges with the awareness that it is okay to be in discomfort. Remember you are building new muscle. The more you put yourself in discomfort zones, the more emotional muscle you build. Continue to seek out and put yourself in discomfort zones. Go back to school, learn a new language, try out for a play, or volunteer to give a presentation at work. As you continue to exercise your emotional muscle through new experiences, you build emotional muscle.

The feeling of accomplishment you felt when you achieved a physical goal such as losing weight or getting in shape applies to developing emotional muscle. You can feel good about having met the challenge of a new emotional situation. You have grown. As in physical fitness programs, you are stretching, developing, and strengthening the most important muscles you have, your emotional muscles.

When you try to create physical change, you receive physical discomfort. Just as you build a physical muscle in your body, you must build emotional muscle in your mind.

When you try to create an emotional change, you will receive emotional discomfort. You may even have pain in parts of your mind you didn't even know you had. If you fail to stretch and build emotional muscle, they become weaker and weaker. If they go unexercised, they become harder to access. Keep putting yourself in discomfort zones and build emotional muscle.

CAVES

It seems that any group has at least one person who is against virtually everything. They sit in the back of the room at meetings flexing their power by suffocating any new thoughts or ideas. They can't get over their own fears and weaknesses so they do whatever they can to bring the group down to their level. These people are like CAVES. They are dark, foul, make it hard to breathe, have no light and lack value.

CAVE stands for Citizens Against Virtually Everything. These CAVES have power for one reason, someone gave it to them. CAVES attempt to ruin groups with negativity and opposition to all change. They can be heard saying things like, "we must do that, because we've always done it that way," or "that will never work," and even, "that's a stupid idea."

Being against virtually everything is worse than doing nothing. CAVES not only harm themselves; they try to harm others. When they should be helping, CAVES are intentionally spreading doom and gloom.

Think of the CAVES you know. They have victim mentalities and are waiting for a miracle like the lottery to save them from a dreadful life. They are in a constant state of suffering and want you to share in their misery.

Beware of Citizens Against Virtually Everything because they alienate group members and attract other CAVES.

Everyone has at least one CAVE standing in their way. The more involved you get, the more CAVES you will run into. The quicker you realize this, the better off you'll be. To loosen the grip CAVES have gained, first identify them, and then do whatever it takes to remove their power. Don't idly stand by and allow them to bring down your group.

It seems that any group has at least one Citizen Against Virtually Everything. They speak out and constantly attack. This article is not intended to turn CAVES into positive people. That takes more time and effort than I care to spend. What this article is intended to do is to make you aware of Citizens Against Virtually Everything and stop you from giving them power.

Stop giving CAVES power in your group and put them back in to their hole.

Connecting

In this day and age, people are making amazing amounts of virtual connections through networks like Twitter, Linkedin, and Facebook. While the virtual world is all good, real world connecting is still where it's at. Computers and cell phones are fantastic tools, but don't let them replace connecting with someone in person. The ability to connect in person gives you a significant competitive advantage.

Connecting with people (customers, colleagues, bosses, employees, and even total strangers) is the process of building relationships of mutual trust and understanding. Making connections does not mean that you share the same point of view; you just have to be able to understand where they are coming from. Accepting differences is a must if you want to be a good connector.

Connecting online has become easy. So easy in fact, that we are forgetting what it takes to connect in person. Where speed is essential to online connecting, the opposite is true face to face. To connect face to face, you must slow down and take the initiative to go beyond technology in order to form solid connections. You should create an environment that is conducive to connecting. Connecting is determined not just by how you feel, but how you make others feel. The best way to put others at ease is to be at ease yourself. To connect face to face, it takes a significant investment of time and effort.

As with any other investment, connections can improve lives. Connecting in real life builds valuable relationships that lead to opportunities. In this day and age, it is a must to turn your virtual connections into real world connections. The more real world connections you can make, the more you can maximize the opportunities in those relationships. Real world connections are the social fabric that supports us, and the ability to make those connections gives you a significant advantage.

Happiness or Bust

Happiness — the pursuit of so many. In fact, Americans are known as those who live for "Life, liberty, and the pursuit of happiness."

But so many Americans seem without happiness. Why is this? Is happiness truly elusive or do we simply not know how to take hold of it? It is my contention that happiness is yours for the taking. That is, anyone can be happy if they choose to be — and if they know how to get it.

So what does it take to bring us happiness? Here are a few thoughts to get you on your way.

Do not try to control circumstances. One of the biggest "happiness busters" I see is from circumstances that have gone awry. People experience (and wallow in) frustration because their mind-set, whether they know it or not, is that they should be, somehow, able to control circumstances. But, let's get this straight. You can't! So the first thing you can do to give yourself happiness is to stop trying to control, or take responsibility for, circumstances that are outside of your control! Understand that there is only one thing you can control in this world and that is yourself. You can't control the weather, other drivers, your kids or spouse, or anything for that matter outside of your own beliefs, thoughts, attitudes, and actions. Focus all of your attention on developing yourself and doing what is right — controlling yourself while letting what will happen, happen — and you will find happiness opening up within you.

Courage

Courage is one of the most rewarding personal attributes a person can have. It is a spirit that enables you to confront uncertainty. Courage is not the absence of fear; it is acting in spite of it. It takes courage to realize your goals. No one is born with courage; it must be cultivated. Be courageous in your life and in your pursuit of the person you want to be.

Courage must be cultivated. You develop courage the same way you develop any other skill, by doing. By taking action toward your goals, in spite of fear, your courage grows. Courage is a by-product of going after what you want and becoming the person you want to be. Harvest courage from every opportunity that life offers you. As your courage grows, your fears wither. Luckily, the world gives you plenty of opportunities to practice.

Courage is a crucial ingredient in relationships. You give and draw courage from others. It takes courage to tell a friend what they need to hear, not what they want to hear. It takes courage to speak up against prejudice at the local hang out. It takes courage to stand up to an injustice at work. The absence of courage opens the door to fear. Each time you demonstrate the courage to speak up, stand up, or move forward, you close the door on fear.

Move toward the things you fear and the fear diminishes and your courage increases. When you build enough courage, you take control of your own destiny. Courage is needed to take the risks that can lead to a brighter future. Courageous people step to the front, rather than stepping back when opportunities come their way. When you cultivate the courage to become the kind of person that you want to be, you uncover and develop your greatest talents. Cultivate courage.

Discomfort Zone

I'm sure you've heard the phrase "step outside of your comfort zone" for self improvement. I never liked that phrase. Getting out of your comfort zone is like walking over to the pool and sticking your big toe in to test the temperature. If you want to improve, you're going to have to do more than just stick your big toe in the water. You have to run over to the pool and cannonball in. Does that make a splash in your mind? Don't just step outside your comfort zone; seek out and jump into the Discomfort Zone.

Discomfort Zones are areas of life you avoid. They're easy to identify but hard to face. Just thinking about them gives you an unpleasant feeling in your stomach. Discomfort Zones can be physical, emotional, cultural, intellectual, and financial. It is uncomfortable to exercise, for example, but comfortable to sit on the couch. It is uncomfortable to apply for a new job; it is comfortable to stay in your current position. It is uncomfortable to forgive; it is comfortable to hold a grudge. It is uncomfortable to be accountable; it is comfortable to blame someone else. It is uncomfortable to tell the truth and often comfortable to lie.

You are comfortable where you feel safe, but understand that being safe is a dangerous place. The pursuit of comfort is like a drug that continually tempts you to avoid pain. Comfort leads to mediocre performance, poor relationships, and disappointment. Your comfort zone is boring and dulls your senses. Being comfortable sucks the life right out of you. It's a natural law of nature that all things in the universe are either living or dying a little more each day. If you're always comfortable, you're existing, not living.

If your comfort zone is dangerous, being uncomfortable must be safe. What? Isn't the Discomfort Zone painful? Yes, and embarrassing, frightening, and traumatic. It is an emotional place full of surprises which keeps you edgy. You perform at higher levels and increase creativity, resourcefulness, and inspiration. Ask the most successful people you know and you'll find that rather than avoid pain, they accept it. They'll tell you that pain equals growth, and the benefits far outweigh the discomfort.

When you step outside your comfort zone, the very moment you feel pain, it is too easy to go back to where you were. This is why people fail to improve themselves. They are unwilling to accept pain. Once you jump into a Discomfort Zone, there is no stepping back to comfort. When you realize this concept, you become willing to do what others won't. You become a Discomfort Zoner. You embrace discomfort until it becomes tolerable. Soon the pain subsides. You enjoy the benefits, and the pain is forgotten.

Jumping into the Discomfort zone is not a nuisance, but a necessity. To improve your life, you must jump in and stake your claim. If you don't, you're going to be stuck where you are, standing by the edge of the pool sticking your big toe in to test the temperature. Think about it. Is that where you want to be?

Eye Contact

Next to breathing, smiling is the most important thing you can do. To produce a powerful weapon, combine that smile with eye contact. When you do, you build a communication weapon so powerful it has been outlawed in elevators, airports, and used car lots across the country. Eye contact can determine the difference between a successful encounter and one that leads to embarrassment and even rejection. Eye contact shows confidence and builds trust. Eye contact (with a smile) is the quickest, easiest, least-expensive way to get what you want.

Eye contact is the number one form of nonverbal communication, and the best way to get someone's attention. It is the foundation of communication and a terrific step toward first impressions, friendships, and business relationships. It's been said that the eyes are the mirrors of the soul. Your eyes speak your true feelings, and when you are excited about what you are saying the confidence shines through.

Trust and eye contact are very closely related. Failing to make eye contact causes suspicion. The eyes speak mutely, but they speak truly. Not making or avoiding eye contact sends a message that you may be shifty, sneaky, guilty, bashful, or frightened. If you have a habit of looking away while listening, it shows lack of interest. Failing to maintain eye contact while speaking, at a minimum, shows a lack of confidence in what you are saying and, at a maximum, sends the indication that you are not trustworthy.

Eye contact is crucial to establishing a human connection and a sense of trust between individuals. While using eye contact, be careful not to stare, squint, or blink your eyes rapidly. Consider how long you look into someone's eyes when you speak. Eye contact expresses intimacy, and as a direct glance becomes longer, the feelings become more intense. Because of the intimacy and openness involved with eye contact, some people have trouble with it.

Eye contact does not come naturally to everyone. In fact, many people have difficulty looking someone in the eye. If you find yourself nervous about looking people directly in the eye, start small and keep working at improving. With practice, you will become more comfortable with using direct eye contact and you will enjoy the benefits.

Eye contact is the quickest, easiest, least-expensive way to get what you want. It is the communication foundation. Eye contact shows confidence and builds trust like no other communication weapon available to humankind. Eye contact is unequaled in importance. Look them in the eye and smile.

Focus On Your Strengths

Has anyone ever told you to focus on your weaknesses? As far back as I can remember, family members, teachers, coaches, and friends have told me to improve upon my weaknesses. As a kid in sports, I was told over and over that I was too slow and needed to get faster. So I worked my tail off to fix my sloth footedness. Guess what? I'm still slow.

Sure, I got a little faster, but never enough to notice a difference. Imagine if I would have invested that time I spent trying to get faster in the library? Working on weaknesses is one of the weakest things you can do! Don't waste precious time and effort struggling to get just a tiny bit better at something that just doesn't, and never will, come naturally. Focus on your strengths, not your weaknesses. You'll get much better results and be happier.

We've been taught and conditioned to concentrate on weaknesses. In my seminars, I have people list their strengths and weaknesses on paper. Many have a difficult time coming up with 5 or 10 strengths and then need extra sheets of paper to list all of their weaknesses (try it sometime, I dare you). If you allow your weaknesses to become the focus of your life, you'll go to the grave with unused talents.

Don't confuse a weakness with acquiring the skills or knowledge you lack to achieve a goal. Weakness, in this definition, is an inability to perform something well that cannot be corrected through training (sloth footedness). These weaknesses are difficult and frustrating to you no matter how hard you work. It's best to understand that you're not good at everything — and you never will be.

Focusing on weaknesses spends an enormous amount of time and energy, often with very little return. It is more effective to invest in building strengths because you can improve upon them faster than you can your weaknesses. Work around your weaknesses by hiring or partnering with someone whose strength is your weakness. Working on improving strengths leads to excellence. Fixing weaknesses only leads to mediocrity.

Imagine what your life would be like if you focused on what you do well. You are not good at everything and you never will be. Improve upon your strengths and work around your weaknesses. Working on your weaknesses is the weakest thing you can do. You'll receive a far greater return and be much happier by focusing on your strengths.

Get Organized

As expectations and demands rise, life can be overwhelming. Many people struggle through days that have them rushing around and running out of time. Stress levels have skyrocketed as we cram more into each day. If you feel overwhelmed, it is time to take control and get organized. Despite all of life's demands, you can control your life if you get organized.

If you don't know where to begin organizing, pick one small part of your life and start there. Work on keeping that small part organized and over time it will become a habit. If you are always looking for your keys, put some hooks on the wall near the door and make it a habit of putting your keys on the hooks. After a couple of months of putting your keys on the hooks, that part of your life will be organized and you will begin to look for the next small area to organize. Putting your keys on a hook may seem insignificant, but this small success will boost your confidence and lead to more success.

One of the simpliest ways to help the organizational process is to put stuff back. Once you've found a place for something, when you use it, put it back right away. Develop the habit of putting it back as soon as you're finished using it. Don't set it on the table or the couch and think to yourself that you'll put it away later. You'll end up with little things sitting all over your house.

Don't expect to get organized overnight. That would be impossible. Try to make one small change every month or so until it becomes second nature. It is important to develop good habits. When you start organizing small parts of your life, you won't feel overwhelmed and stressed out. You'll take back control of your life rather than letting it control you. Start small and get organized.

Get Results

Get results! Like it or not, you are judged on what you do, not what you are capable of doing or what you say you will do. As you begin to look at your life ahead, it's important to inventory your accomplishments. Look at your results and determine if they match up to where you want to be. Results show a clear picture. Results never lie. Your rewards in life are based on your results, not potential results.

We live in a world of uncertainty and one certain way to measure success is to measure results. I was the classic underachiever in grade school. I sat with my mom and dad through countless parent-teacher conferences that went something like this:

> "Matt has worlds of potential;
>> but, he doesn't pay attention;
>> but, he doesn't do his homework;
>> but, he doesn't concentrate;
>> but, he talks too much."

You get the picture. It took a number of tough lessons, including a near repeat of the fifth grade, for me to learn that potential does not get a person very far. What I was *capable* of doing and what I was *actually* doing were worlds apart. It took two tough parents and a very patient eighth-grade teacher before I figured out that I was predicting my future by my results. My potential didn't get me squat.

Results define character, beliefs, and what you are really made of. Your results are a reflection of how you think, talk, and what you do on a daily basis. If you are not getting the results you want, it is from lack of performance. Either you don't know how to perform or you don't want to perform. If you want different results, you need to do things differently. If you keep doing the same thing over and over again and expect different results, you're insane. It's not that hard to do something different. Do you remember what you did yesterday? Well, if you don't like the results you got yesterday, change what you do today.

Getting results is absolutely necessary to keep you moving forward. Are your results moving you toward your goals? It is pretty simple, life doesn't care how many hours you worked or how busy you are, it cares about results. Did you revise your resume? Quit smoking? Have you lost those ten pounds? Have you paid down your debt? Rewards come from results, not potential. Getting results is the most important thing you do. Figure out what you've been doing and, if you don't like the results, do something different.

Harmful If Swallowed

Forgiveness is giving up resentment and bitterness against another (or yourself). One of the most important, yet thorniest, things you will ever do in life is forgiving someone who has wounded you. Refusing to forgive is toxic to your life. Nelson Mandela put it this way, "Hating someone is drinking poison and expecting the other person to die from it." By forgiving, you rid your body of that poison. Forgive others who have hurt you, not because they deserve it, but because you deserve it.

The greatest benefit of forgiveness goes to the person giving it, not the one receiving it. When you forgive, you literally cleanse your body of contamination. You are freeing yourself from the hatred you've been swallowing.

The cost of refusing to forgive is high. It affects your attitude, how you treat people and even your health. When you refuse to forgive, you get angry, bitter, and stressed. You become more prone to numerous ailments such as ulcers, heart problems, anxiety attacks, and cancer. Study after study shows that one of the keys to happiness is to develop a habit of letting go of past hurts.

Some people get so angry, they are unable or unwilling to consider forgiveness as an option. Want proof? Just listen or watch the news. Forgiveness is a choice. When you say, "I can't forgive that person," what you're really saying is, "I'm choosing not to forgive that person." Forgiveness does not mean that you condone, forget, ignore, or accept what occurred; you are simply forgiving them and choosing to move on. You may not think you are ready to forgive, but do it anyway. That anger, bitterness, and stress is lethal.

Hatred towards others is harmful if swallowed. Forgiveness frees you from contamination. It is a virtue of which the world has too little. When you finally decide to let go of past hurts, you empower yourself. By deciding to forgive others, you find peace. Think of one person right now who has wounded you. Can you see that person? Now, forgive them. You deserve it!

Help Yourself First

Help yourself first! If you work harder on helping yourself than you do on anything else, there is no limit to how much value you can create. When you help yourself first, you become more interesting, creative, and productive. Help yourself first and you will have what it takes to truly make a difference in people's lives. Besides, you can't effectively help others until you first help yourself.

If you are always putting others first, you send a message of insecurity and low self esteem. People will take advantage of you which leads to resentment. It is unhealthy to bury your own self-interest in favor of someone else's. If you don't help yourself first, you become damaged goods emotionally, physically, intellectually, and spiritually. By not taking care of yourself, you are the least help to others because you are less tolerant and less understanding.

Secure you own oxygen mask first, just as the airline stewardess tells you before take-off. Once you have your mask secure, as the old analogy goes, then help others around you. You may find it hard to breathe if you always help others before you help yourself. If you can't breathe, you're not much help to anyone.

This does not mean do not help others, it is actually the opposite. The more you help yourself, the more you are able to help others. You are at your best when you take care of you first. Even as a baby, you helped yourself first. You simply were not happy until you got what you needed. When you help yourself first, you show that you are important which leads to meaningful relationships.

The most important thing you will ever do is take care of yourself. If you aren't doing it now, you must begin the process of working harder on yourself than you do on anything else. When you help yourself first, you become the best you can be. When you're the best you can be, that's when you provide the most help to others. By taking care of your own needs first, you are able to add the most value to others. This approach to life can make a world of positive difference. Help yourself first.

In The Moment

Live in the moment. Lives are so complex and so full of things to do that it is easy to let moments slip by without notice. If you're not in the moment, you're either thinking about the past or the future. You cannot operate from the past or the future because the past is history and the future is mystery. You can be in the moment!

At any given time, you are smack dab in the middle of to do's, tasks, burdens, problems, annoyance, and responsibilities. Moments become lost amid all the confusion and clutter. Your focus is on what needs to be done this minute rather than what you can do with each moment. To be in the moment, you cannot be thinking about what you have done or what you are going to do.

If you are dwelling on the past, you are not in the moment. It may be tempting to think about the past because it was wonderful or awful. However, whatever the past was, it's gone. You cannot operate from the future either, because it's a mystery. Do not spend your time fantasizing about winning the lottery. You should learn from the past and plan for your future while keeping your attention on the moment. Don't miss what is happening now because you were too busy looking back on the past or forward to the future.

Kids live in the moment. I know the cutest little two-year-old girl. She'll laugh or cry any time and return to normal without ever thinking about it again. She doesn't care what happened 5 minutes ago let alone what happened with the stock market yesterday. She's not overly concerned with the price of gas or who will be our next president. All she cares about are the bubbles (bugs) or savoring her mouthful of fruit.

Our dog, Murphy, lives in the moment. As I'm writing this, she is in the front yard pointing at a mourning dove. I've seen her do that for hours. She is concentrating so hard on the moment, everything else in the world disappears. She is not thinking about what she did or didn't have for breakfast or about her upcoming appointment at the vet. She is living in the moment. We only need to look at children or pets for examples and inspiration of living in the moment.

Being in the moment enhances the value of your life. Try to be aware of what is going on in this moment and recognize the importance. I don't think it is possible to be in the moment all of the time. There will always be times when you think about the past or worry about the future. Build your life out of the moments you are given, and be careful not to let them slip by into the shadows and become forgotten and lost forever. Within each moment lies the essence of life. With practice, you can learn to live in the moment longer and enjoy life more.

Influence by Example

Do as I say, not as I do. How many times have you heard that? Unless you're six years old, that theory just doesn't cut it. For example, if I told you it is important to be positive and every time you saw me I was in a bad mood, what would you think? When the message (be positive) doesn't match the action (bad mood), you believe the action. To successfully influence others, you must influence by example.

Influence is the power to affect someone or something. It is the ability to change conduct, thoughts, or decisions. There are many strategies available to influence people. You can influence others through words, generosity, persistence, rewards, punishments, gimmicks, and emotional pulls. The ultimate way, however, is influencing by example.

Assume right now that people learn behavior by imitating others. The more uncertain someone is, the more likely they will follow others' actions. People are influenced more or less depending on the situation, and it is the behavior of others that gives insight into how to act. Being aware of this makes you more conscious about setting a good example.

While you may have control or authority over other people, that doesn't necessarily mean you can easily influence them. If you tell people to show up to work on time and you are often late, what happens? If you expect them to show up on time you should, by example, show up on time. If you tell people what to do and don't do it yourself, they may not even listen to, let alone do what you want them to do.

Your example is what's important when influencing people. To be successful, copy successful people and fashion yourself into the kind of person that others will emulate. As people watch you and see your successes, they will be influenced by your example. Actions speak louder than words. The "Do As I Say, Not As I Do" Theory just doesn't work. When the message doesn't match the action, people believe the action.

Integrity

How do you act when no one is looking? Do you speed up and slip through that yellow light? Do you throw your wrapper on the ground? Do you tell that little bitty lie? Each day your integrity is tested. Some tests are very big while others seem less important.

Although most of your daily tests may not be big, your integrity is determined as much by the little tests as it is by the big ones. How you act when no one is looking exemplifies your integrity.

Integrity means putting character over personal gain. It is sticking to your own personal code of conduct and being accountable for your actions. Someone with integrity doesn't compromise their beliefs. You know where that person stands. Lies and manipulation are not part of their code. Having integrity is a lot like being pregnant. Either you're pregnant, or you're not.

There's no such thing as being a little bit pregnant. There is also no such thing as having a little bit of integrity. Either you have it, or you don't.

Having integrity is not a matter of convenience. People are quick to judge and criticize others who lack integrity and then are just as prone to compromise their own code of conduct when it's convenient. Showing up late, cheating on a test, lying, and even internet shopping for personal items on company time all show lack of integrity. When you compromise your personal code of conduct, integrity is lost.

If you are a person with integrity, your life will be free of confusion. You have nothing to cover up and no guilt. Integrity allows you to hold your head up high and look people in the eye. When you stick to what you know is right, you win. When you live with integrity, you succeed.

Making choices based on your personal code of conduct can be a struggle. The freedom that comes from making the right choices — both small and large — is worth the struggle.

Commitment to integrity is a vital part of life. Alan Simpson put it this way, "If you have integrity, nothing else matters. If you don't have integrity, nothing else matters." Integrity isn't just what you do; it is who you are and how you act when no one is looking.

Internal GPS

If you get lost while driving, what do you do? You grab a map or better yet, the GPS system to guide you in the right direction. A GPS system does not come standard with every vehicle. Lucky for you, every person comes equipped with an internal GPS. This "gut feeling" helps guide your decisions and actions. Your internal GPS is indispensable. Still, many people go about their daily lives never connecting to it. It is essential to listen to and trust your internal GPS.

This internal GPS is your very own personal guide. It is intended to help you find solutions that can save you time and create opportunities. It is a "gut feeling" that's impossible to explain, but you just know. You know something without knowing exactly how you know it. Many people hear the message, yet dismiss it. How often have you felt you were making the wrong decision, but you made it anyway based on logic? Your internal GPS can be difficult to trust because there are no guarantees or tangible evidence. It is easy to learn to ignore it and look for answers elsewhere.

You cannot command your internal GPS or use it at will. It surfaces spontaneously and taps you on the shoulder. Often, people get scared of their internal GPS because it can lead to major changes and tough choices. Your internal GPS isn't always right and you should check it with available information. Just because it isn't always right doesn't mean you should stop listening to it. Your internal GPS is a great tool to consider when making decisions.

Your body gives you a tremendous amount of useful, intuitive information. That "gut feeling" or "hunch" is one of the most valuable and under-used skills in the human tool box. Reconnect with your internal GPS and listen when it tells you something. Look inside for the solutions and begin producing extraordinary results, in less time, with less effort and much more fun. Listen to your internal GPS and trust it to help guide your decisions. I have a "gut feeling" you'll like it.

Life Balance

Life is like riding a bicycle. To keep your balance you must keep moving. Albert Einstein

Balance in life is important. It is only after finding balance that you can successfully contribute to your family, friends, and community. According to Einstein, balance is about moving (progress). Progress also comes with the risk of falling. Find your balance, not someone else's vision of balance for you. If you're happy, you're balanced. After all, it's your bicycle.

Think about a time when you felt really happy about life; I'll bet it was a time when you were passionate and completely involved in something. It could have been a career, family, spiritual, community, or a personal area of your life. You were doing what you wanted; maybe it was mastering a sport, losing weight, volunteering, or doing a project.

Sure, you felt happy, but were you really balanced?

Life balance is essential, but be realistic about balance in the quest for progress. Progress first requires imbalance. When you're passionate about something and pursue it, then almost by default, other areas of your life will get less attention and might even be entirely neglected. A skillful artist, for example, is consumed by his/her craft and spends little time on anything else. It's unlikely that any remarkable piece of work was created while the artist pursued a state of balance.

Your main focus at any particular point in time takes away from your ability to pay attention to other areas of your life. No matter how hard you attempt to achieve balance, there will inevitably be competition between different areas of your life. This competition keeps you moving.

Your life is dynamic, not static. As a unique person, the important areas of your life constantly change. You fall in love, get married, have children, you may get divorced, land a new job (or lose one), someone you love gets sick, or you develop entirely new interests. At different stages in your life, different areas compete for your attention, and it's only natural to focus on what is most important at that moment. However, when you feel a tilt that might cause a fall, it's time to check your balance.

It's unreasonable to expect your life to be in perfect balance. Instead of trying to balance all areas at any one time, acknowledge that progress requires imbalance. Don't do enough to make others happy, do what it takes to balance your bike. If you're truly happy, then aren't you balanced? It's your bicycle. Find your balance and keep moving. It will take you on the journey of your life.

Lifelong Improvement

The cornerstone of happiness and success is lifelong self improvement. Continual improvement gives you the edge mentally, physically, and emotionally. It's the learning of new skills, new concepts, and new experiences that keeps you evolving. You are either living or dying a little more each day. Your mission in life, should you choose to accept it, is to commit to lifelong self improvement. If you're improving, you're living.

Self improvement can be found in formal and informal learning environments. How you improve is not as important as having the mindset to improve. Sometimes improving will be easy and other times it will be darn hard. There are many areas in your life that you can improve upon. Maybe you want to be a better friend, spouse, parent, and business person. How about improving your health, education, finances, emotional, and spiritual self? You can read a book, meditate, change your diet, take a class, exercise, volunteer, earn a degree, or attend training. You can be better, do something better, increase your awareness, learn something new, or even create radical change if you wish.

You cannot control the world around you; you can only control yourself. Engaging in lifelong improvement enables you to embrace change rather than endure it.

When you improve yourself, you feel better; you are more willing to take risks and accept challenges.

Remember, self improvement does not stop when you leave the classroom. There is an opportunity to improve when you read, see, hear, and observe. Invest in your future by ongoing self improvement. It is the very heart of life. Make it your mission to improve and evolve. If you're improving, you're living.

Mirror, Mirror

Success often depends on how well a person can connect with others. Some people find connecting easy to do, while others have to really work at it. On a basic level, people are drawn to people when their body language (gestures, tone of voice, facial expressions, eye contact, and so on) is similar. One way to appear similar to others is to mirror their behaviors.

Few techniques will connect you more effectively than mirroring. To mirror another person, you simply pick a behavior you wish to mirror and then copy that behavior. If you choose to mirror an arm movement for example, when the person moves their arms, wait a few seconds and then move yours to the same position. If they lean forward to tell you something, you lean forward to meet them. When they sit back to take a sip of their drink, you pause, then follow suit. There are a wide range of behaviors that can be mirrored, for example:

•	Body posture	•	Hand gestures
•	Blink rate	•	Facial expression
•	Energy level	•	Breathing rate
•	Head tilt	•	Vocal qualities
•	Key phrases		(pace, rhythm, tonality)

Basically, anything that you can observe, you can mirror. At your next social gathering, take a look around and see the examples of mirroring. Mirroring is not the same as mimicry. It should be subtle and respectful. Friends often mirror each other unconsciously. When done successfully, few people will ever notice. Mirroring allows individuals to be comfortable and even puts complete strangers at ease.

Mirroring gives you a head start toward making the connections that are essential for success. Mirroring is easy and it works. When you use it properly, you'll improve the connections you make with virtually anyone.

Nation of Spectators

American's obsession with sports and reality shows has moved us from being a nation of doers to a nation of spectators. As spectators, we sit in front of the TV and watch others take action. According to the A.C. Nielsen Co., the average American watches more than four hours of TV each day. That equals twenty-eight hours per week and two full months of TV per year. Watching TV has become America's most popular pastime and biggest time waster.

The foremost complaint I hear on a regular basis is lack of time. No one has enough time to take action on the dreams they want to accomplish. If that sounds like your life, maybe you're spending too much time on things that don't matter, like TV. Time management is a myth. You cannot *manage* time; you can only control what you do with the time you have. Everyone has the exact same amount of time. What separates the doers from the spectators is action. The simplest, easiest, and cheapest way to take action on your dreams is to turn off the TV. Almost anything else you do is more productive than watching TV.

Here are a few tips to reduce the amount of time you watch TV:

- Move your TV to a less prominent location
- Keep the TV off during meals
- Designate certain days of the week as TV-free days
- Do not use TV as a reward
- Listen to music or the radio for background music
- Cancel your cable subscription.

I threw out my TV in May of 2006 and immediately noticed a substantial difference. I began to find time to go to the gym, read those books, visit my grandma, and write these articles. By watching less TV, I made time to take action. I know you're thinking that you don't possibly watch four hours of TV per day, but I dare you to add it up.

You start out watching a half hour of *Headline News* in the morning, then a half hour of *Sports Center*. You catch the season premier of *American Idol* or *Grey's Anatomy*, and finally, you close the night with *Myth Busters* or *The World's Deadliest Catch*.

Don't get me wrong, I still enjoy movies and a good game on occasion. Imagine what your life can be like with an extra two, three, or four hours per day.

If you've become a spectator rather than a doer, learn to distinguish between what is important and what is not. If you think TV is important, by all means continue watching four hours per day. If you never take action on your dreams, please don't use the excuse that you didn't have time. Television is a big time waster. Turn off the TV and turn on life. When you do, you'll find the time to take action on your dreams.

Practice What You Teach

Everyone dishes out advice from time to time. We tell our spouses, friends, and even complete strangers what they must do, or should do, or how to do it. Being a speaker, I certainly dish out my fair share. I've learned that if I'm dishing it out, I better practice what I teach. It would be pretty dim-witted of me to give a speech about the importance of having a positive attitude and then flip someone off on the drive home. If you want credibility and you want people to listen to your advice, you better practice what you teach.

To "teach" is to tell others the right way to do something; to "practice" is to do the thing yourself. You "practice what you teach" when you yourself do something the same way you tell others to do it. Example: You can't warn your kids about the dangers of smoking and then have a cigarette. Your actions (what you do) should always be consistent with your words (what you say). You should strive to do the things you advise others to do.

Practicing what you teach is repeatedly ignored. Have you ever noticed that when others continually tell you what you should or must do, they often don't follow their own advice? You may even hear them say something like, do as I say, not as I do. People will only listen to your advice after they watch you demonstrate it. If you continue to offer advice to someone without practicing what you teach, that advice may feel more like an insult than a genuine attempt to help.

If you're going to dish out advice to others (from the stage or not), you had better make sure that you are practicing what you teach.

Touch

Touch is a form of communication that exchanges energy and builds foundations for relationships. When done appropriately, touch makes you appear warmer, more friendly, kinder, and memorable. Touch helps you communicate a clear message and, most importantly, makes life meaningful. When it comes to effective communication, a single touch can make all the difference.

Touch is the first and most primal form of all senses. You experience touch in the womb and it is one of the last senses you lose before death. Babies who receive little to no touch can grow depressed, stop eating, and die. Touch relieves stress, makes you happier, and keeps you healthier. People require touch. It is a basic need of life.

In our fast-paced lives, however, we often disregard the importance of physical touch. Many organizations and policies discourage touch as a form of communication. A "touchy" person is often regarded as unprofessional or an invader of personal space. Our society is becoming overly cautious about the use of touch as communication.

Clearly, different forms of touch are more appropriate at some times and places than at others. For example, you probably want to avoid hugging strangers in public restrooms.

When it feels right and appropriate, touch is an excellent way to communicate a message. People have a universal need to connect with others. Ritualized forms of touch are effective ways to satisfy that basic need. Familiar forms of touch are handshakes, hugs, high fives, knuckles, and a pat on the back. Touch can say as much or more than words.

You should practice touching people gently on the hand or forearm to make a point, to emphasize a statement, or to express appreciation. You will be amazed at how touch affects people in such a positive way. Continue expressing your affection and appreciation of others by patting them on the shoulder or back, or even putting your arm around them.

Touch makes life meaningful and is a reminder that love, safety, and caring exists. When it comes to effective communication, a simple touch can make all the difference.

Trust

Do you start relationships with trust or mistrust? Trust is acceptance of something as true or reliable without being able to verify it. When you trust someone, you expect them to do what they say they will do. Mistrust is questioning trust and believing there is a hidden agenda. Trust is the most important factor in the success of relationships.

Starting relationships with trust (rather than mistrust) lets you be ready to derive maximum benefit. Trust leads to accomplishments that are otherwise not possible. Taking people at their word and giving them the benefit of the doubt provides a big advantage in relationship building. When you trust others, you increase their value. People who are trusted tend to live up to those expectations and do their very best to not let that trust fail. Living and operating each day is a matter of trusting others. Trust is the glue for successful relationships.

So often, people start with mistrust rather than trust. Mistrusting others creates fear and anxiety resulting in more mistrust. Mistrust sets everyone up for failure and prepares you be inclined to pass criticism and judgement. Mistrust grows steadily and you may become guarded and second guess everything. Relationships are damaged, often nothing can change or repair that damage. It is an interesting thing, that when you mistrust someone, they will often live down to those expectations as well.

Even though trust brings vulnerability, it is essential for successful relationships. It is unfortunate if you cannot start relationships with trust because of past experiences. It is true that starting with trust leaves you open for hurt and there will always be people who will take advantage of that trust. It is much better to start with trust and give people the benefit of the doubt. If you repeatedly start relationships with mistrust, you may find yourself very lonely.

Urgent vs. Important

Is urgency the norm in your life? Is everything an emergency? Are you overworked and overwhelmed by things that should have been done yesterday. The urgency of the moment has a way of preempting the important. The eternal putting out of fires leads to feeling like your life is out of control. If you feel that way, stop, breathe (in through the nose and out through the mouth), then determine the difference between urgent and important. Invest your time on the important.

Urgent activities are crises that require immediate attention. You react to emergencies and push aside important matters until they escalate and become emergencies, at which point you have yet another crisis. The number of urgent tasks you deal with each day correlates directly to the amount of stress you experience. This urgency-induced stress compromises your health and leads to overall poor performance.

Everything is not urgent! When you go to the emergency room, you believe your situation is urgent. However, the doctors don't allow you to define urgency. There would be chaos if they did. Doctors prioritize patients based on the importance of their conditions. Patients with life-threatening problems are attended to first. If your emergency can wait without further harm, you wait.

To ease your urgency-induced stress, learn to distinguish clearly between what is urgent and what is important. Quit responding to urgent tasks faster than you do important matters. Prioritize and do what's most important first. Practice discipline and concentration without submitting to moods and circumstances. By being proactive, rather than reactive, you are able to focus on activities that produce significant results.

Urgent activities will never disappear. Recognize that urgent activities are usually associated with the achievement of someone else's goals rather than your own. When everything is urgent, you get caught up in being busy all of the time and are at the mercy of things that are not the most important. To be happy and successful, invest time on the important matters which help you achieve your goals. Regain control of your life.

What's Your BFG?

Pick one BFG (Big Fricken Goal) and commit to accomplishing it. Try blowing it out of the water or knocking it out of the park. Go big or go home! How about getting your degree, quitting smoking, doubling your income, losing 100 pounds, or getting out of debt? Those are some Big Fricken Goals! A BFG changes your life! It is huge and outrageous. It shouldn't take you long to figure out a BFG. It'll get you excited and make you nauseous at the same time. There will be lots of uncertainty and doubt associated with your BFG. It will not only make you uncomfortable, it will be painful. Decide on your BFG and give it everything you've got.

Choosing a BFG and going after it will virtually guarantee a brighter future. It quickly advances you to a new level of performance. Your BFG will be a focal point of energy and effort. Smaller goals such as losing five pounds, taking out the garbage, visiting family, or waxing the kitchen floor are necessary, but a BFG is life changing.

Most goals are very incremental. They go up a little each year. The problem with incremental is that it is comfortable. People fail when they become too comfortable.

Setting your goals a smidge higher is not sufficient. Go big and you change forever. Big Fricken Goals will not be achieved by doing the same things you did last year. You must think and work differently than you ever have before. BFGs stimulate progress, ignite passion, and focus the mind. A Big Fricken Goal ensures that you do what's important and breaks you through the clutter of mediocrity and small mindedness. Don't settle for setting your goals just a little higher. Go big and change the world.

I know you're thinking that setting a Big Fricken Goal is unrealistic. That's the Big Fricken point. When you focus on a BFG, you see it in your mind and start imagining what life would be like when you accomplish it. When you can visualize something in your mind, it becomes more realistic.

What happens if you set a BFG and fall short?

What if your BFG is to double your income and you don't quite make it, is that OK?

What if your BFG is to lose 100 pounds and you don't quite make it, is that OK?

Sometimes you have to be unrealistic and overestimate your abilities, or you risk spending your entire life living below your capacity. Living below capacity is what happens to people who never push themselves. They grow mentally weaker and weaker over time, losing more